Axton Nexus

Building Concurrent Web Scraper

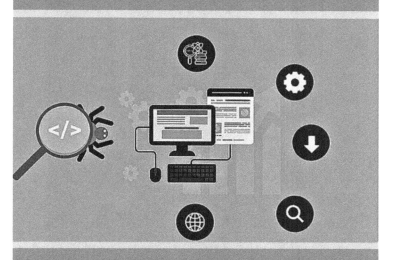

A Hands-On Beginner's Guide to Building
Scalable, Efficient and Reliable Web
Scrapers Using Modern Programming
Techniques

Table Of Content

Disclaimer

The information provided in this book, "Building Concurrent Web Scrapers," is intended for educational and informational purposes only. While every effort has been made to ensure the accuracy and completeness of[1] the content, the author and publisher make no representations or warranties of any kind, express or implied, about the completeness, accuracy, reliability,[2] suitability, or availability with respect to the book or the information, products, services, or related graphics contained in the book for any purpose. Any reliance you place on such information is therefore strictly at your own risk.[3]

Web scraping involves interacting with websites and online services, which are subject to their own terms of service, usage policies, and legal restrictions. It is your responsibility to ensure that your web scraping activities comply with all applicable laws and regulations, as well as the terms of service of the websites you access.

The author and publisher do not condone or encourage any illegal or unethical web scraping activities. The techniques and examples provided in this book should be used responsibly and ethically, respecting the rights of website owners, users, and the broader internet community.

The code examples in this book are provided as illustrations and might require modifications or adaptations to suit your specific needs and the target websites. The author and publisher are not responsible for any errors or omissions in the code or for any consequences arising from the use of the code.

The internet is a dynamic environment, and websites frequently change their structure, content, and security measures. The techniques and information provided in this book might become outdated or less effective over time. It is your responsibility to stay informed about the latest web scraping best practices, legal developments, and ethical considerations.

The author and publisher are not liable for any damages, including but not limited to direct, indirect, incidental, consequential, or punitive damages, arising out of or in connection[4] with the use or misuse of the information or code provided in this book.

This disclaimer is intended to be a comprehensive statement of the author and publisher's limitations of liability. It does not exclude or limit any liability that cannot be excluded or limited under applicable law.

By using this book, you acknowledge that you have read and understood this disclaimer and agree to its terms.

Introduction

In today's data-driven world, the ability to extract meaningful information from the vast expanse of the internet is no longer a luxury, but a necessity. Web scraping, the art of automatically extracting data from websites, has become an indispensable skill for businesses, researchers, and individuals seeking to harness the power of online information.

This book, "Building Concurrent Web Scrapers," serves as your comprehensive guide to mastering the art and science of web scraping. Whether you're a seasoned developer or just starting your coding journey, this book will equip you with the knowledge and skills to build efficient, scalable, and reliable web scrapers.

We'll begin by exploring the fundamental concepts of web scraping, including the underlying web technologies (HTML, CSS, JavaScript) and the ethical considerations that guide responsible data extraction. You'll learn how to use Python and its powerful libraries (requests, Beautiful Soup) to fetch web pages and extract data with precision.

The heart of this book lies in its focus on concurrency, a critical technique for building high-performance web scrapers. You'll discover how to leverage threads, processes, and asynchronous programming to fetch multiple web pages concurrently, dramatically reducing scraping time and maximizing efficiency.

We'll then move into advanced scraping techniques, tackling challenges like scraping dynamic websites with JavaScript rendering, interacting with APIs, and handling AJAX requests and infinite scrolling. You'll learn how to overcome obstacles like rate limits, IP blocking, and CAPTCHAs, ensuring your scrapers remain robust and resilient.

Data handling is another crucial aspect of web scraping. We'll explore techniques for cleaning, transforming, and validating scraped data, ensuring its accuracy and consistency. You'll also learn how to store and manage your data effectively, from simple CSV files to powerful SQL and NoSQL databases.

As your scraping projects grow in complexity, scalability and maintainability become paramount. We'll guide you through designing scalable scrapers that can handle increasing data volumes and changing website structures. You'll also learn best practices for code organization, testing, and debugging, ensuring your scrapers remain maintainable and adaptable over time.

Finally, we'll look towards the future of web scraping, exploring emerging trends like serverless computing, the integration of AI and machine learning, and the evolving landscape of web technologies.

This book is designed to be your companion throughout your web scraping endeavors. With its practical examples, hands-on exercises, and clear explanations, you'll gain the confidence and expertise to build web scrapers that can extract valuable insights from the vast ocean of online data.

Let's begin our exploration of this fascinating and powerful field!

Part I: Foundations of Web Scraping

Chapter 1: Introduction to Web Scraping

What is Web Scraping?

In today's data-driven world, the ability to extract meaningful information from the vast expanse of the internet is a crucial skill. This is where web scraping comes in. Imagine having the power to automatically gather data from websites, transforming unstructured information into organized datasets ready for analysis, visualization, and decision-making. This chapter introduces the core concepts of web scraping, its applications, and the ethical considerations that guide responsible data extraction.

What is Web Scraping?

Web scraping is the automated process of extracting data from websites. Instead of manually copying and pasting information, web scraping uses intelligent software tools to navigate web pages, target specific data points, and store the extracted information in a structured format. Think of it as a specialized robot designed to sift through web pages and collect the data you need.

The Mechanics of Web Scraping

At its core, web scraping involves a series of steps:

1. **Request:** The web scraper sends a request to the website's server, similar to how your web browser requests a page when you type in a URL.
2. **Response:** The server responds by sending the requested web page's content, which is typically in HTML format.
3. **Parsing:** The scraper parses the HTML content, analyzing its structure and identifying the relevant data.
4. **Extraction:** The scraper extracts the desired data, such as product prices, news articles, or contact information.
5. **Storage:** The extracted data is then stored in a structured format, such as a CSV file, a spreadsheet, or a database.

Key Concepts

- **HTML (HyperText Markup Language):** The foundation of web pages. Web scrapers analyze HTML to understand the structure and content of a page.
- **CSS Selectors:** Used to precisely target specific elements within an HTML document, allowing scrapers to pinpoint the data they need.
- **HTTP (HyperText Transfer Protocol):** The protocol that governs communication between web browsers and servers. Scrapers use HTTP to request web pages.

- **Data Formats:** Scrapers handle various data formats, including HTML, XML, and JSON.

Why Web Scraping Matters

Web scraping has become an essential tool for individuals and organizations across various domains. Here are some of its key applications:

- **Price Monitoring:** Track product prices across multiple e-commerce websites to find the best deals or analyze market trends.
- **Market Research:** Gather data on competitors, customer sentiment, and emerging trends.
- **Lead Generation:** Extract contact information from websites to build marketing lists.
- **News Aggregation:** Collect news articles from various sources to stay informed or perform content analysis.
- **Data Analysis:** Acquire data for research projects, statistical analysis, or machine learning model training.
- **Real Estate Analysis:** Gather property listings, prices, and trends from real estate websites.

Ethical and Legal Considerations

While web scraping is a powerful tool, it's important to use it responsibly and ethically. Here are key considerations:

- **Respect Website Terms of Service:** Always check a website's terms of service to ensure that web scraping is permitted.
- **Robots.txt:** Adhere to the instructions in a website's robots.txt file, which specifies which parts of the site should not be scraped.
- **Avoid Overloading Servers:** Make requests at a reasonable rate to avoid putting excessive strain on a website's server.
- **Protect Privacy:** Be mindful of scraping personal data and ensure compliance with privacy regulations.
- **Copyright:** Respect copyright laws and avoid scraping copyrighted content without permission.

By understanding the principles of web scraping and adhering to ethical guidelines, you can harness the power of this technique to extract valuable insights from the web. In the next chapter, we'll explore the essential web technologies that form the foundation of web scraping.

Use Cases and Applications (e.g., price monitoring, market research, data analysis)

Web scraping's ability to efficiently extract data from websites unlocks a wide range of possibilities across diverse fields.[1] Let's explore some of the most common and impactful applications:

1. Price Monitoring and Comparison

E-commerce has revolutionized the way we shop, giving consumers access to a vast array of products and prices.[2] Web scraping plays a crucial role in this landscape by enabling:

- **Price Comparison Websites:** Services like Google Shopping, PriceRunner, and Camelcamelcamel rely on web scraping to gather product information and pricing data from various online retailers.[3] This allows consumers to quickly compare prices and find the best deals.
- **Dynamic Pricing Strategies:** Businesses use web scraping to track competitor pricing, enabling them to adjust their own prices in real-time to remain competitive.[4]
- **Detecting Price Changes:** Track price fluctuations for specific products over time, helping identify trends, sales patterns, or unusual price drops.[5]

2. Market Research and Analysis

Web scraping provides valuable tools for businesses to gather insights into market dynamics, customer sentiment, and competitor activities:[6]

- **Competitive Analysis:** Monitor competitor websites to track product offerings, marketing campaigns, and customer reviews.[7]
- **Brand Monitoring:** Analyze online mentions of a brand or product to understand public perception, identify potential PR crises, and gauge the effectiveness of marketing campaigns.[8]
- **Market Trend Analysis:** Scrape data from industry-specific websites, forums, and social media platforms to identify emerging trends, customer preferences, and new opportunities.[9]

3. Lead Generation and Sales

For businesses seeking to expand their customer base, web scraping can be a powerful tool for identifying and engaging potential leads:[10]

- **Contact Information Extraction:** Scrape websites, online directories, and business listings to gather contact details like email addresses, phone numbers, and social media profiles.[11]
- **Lead Qualification:** Enrich lead data by scraping additional information, such as company size, industry, and job titles, to identify high-potential prospects.[12]
- **Sales Automation:** Integrate web scraping with CRM (Customer Relationship Management)

systems to automate lead generation and sales outreach.[13]

4. News Aggregation and Content Analysis

Staying informed in today's fast-paced world requires efficient access to news and information. Web scraping facilitates:

- **News Aggregators:** Websites and applications that gather news articles from multiple sources rely on web scraping to provide users with a centralized view of current events.[14]
- **Content Analysis:** Researchers and analysts use web scraping to collect large volumes of news articles, blog posts, and social media content for sentiment analysis, trend identification, and topic modeling.[15]
- **Real-time Event Monitoring:** Track news and social media updates related to specific keywords or events to monitor developing situations or identify potential crises.[16]

5. Data Analysis and Machine Learning

Web scraping plays a vital role in acquiring data for various analytical and research purposes:[17]

- **Academic Research:** Gather data from diverse sources to support research projects in fields like social sciences, economics, and linguistics.[18]
- **Machine Learning Model Training:** Scrape large datasets to train machine learning models for tasks like natural language processing, image recognition, and predictive analytics.[19]
- **Business Intelligence:** Extract data from websites and online platforms to generate reports, dashboards, and visualizations that support data-driven decision-making.[20]

6. Other Notable Applications

- **Real Estate:** Gather property listings, pricing data, and market trends from real estate websites.[21]
- **Travel:** Collect flight information, hotel prices, and travel reviews from travel websites.[22]
- **Financial Markets:** Extract financial data, stock prices, and market indicators from financial websites.[23]
- **Academic Research:** Gather data for research projects across various disciplines.[24]

These examples illustrate the versatility and power of web scraping. By automating the process of data extraction, web scraping empowers individuals and organizations to gather valuable insights, make informed decisions, and gain a competitive edge in today's data-driven world.

Web scraping, while a powerful tool, operates within a complex legal and ethical framework.[1] It's crucial to understand these boundaries to ensure your scraping activities are responsible, sustainable, and avoid potential legal pitfalls.

1. Respecting Website Terms of Service (ToS)

Websites often have terms of service that outline how users can interact with their content.[2] These terms may explicitly prohibit or restrict web scraping activities.[3]

- **Review the ToS:** Before scraping a website, carefully review its terms of service. Look for clauses related to data extraction, automated access, and acceptable use.
- **Explicit Prohibitions:** Some websites explicitly forbid any form of automated data collection.[4] Respect these restrictions to avoid legal challenges.
- **Rate Limits and Access Restrictions:** ToS may specify limits on the frequency of requests or restrict access to certain parts of the website.

Adhere to these limits to avoid being blocked or flagged as a malicious actor.

2. Adhering to robots.txt

The robots.txt file is a text file that website owners use to instruct web robots (like search engine crawlers and web scrapers) about which parts of their site should not be accessed.

- **Locating robots.txt:** You can usually find a website's robots.txt file at the root of its domain (e.g., www.example.com/robots.txt).
- **Understanding Directives:** robots.txt uses directives like Disallow to specify which URLs or sections of a website should not be accessed.
- **Respecting Instructions:** Always check the robots.txt file before scraping and strictly adhere to its directives. Ignoring these instructions can lead to your scraper being blocked or even legal action in some cases.[5]

3. Avoiding Harm and Overloading Servers

Web scraping should be conducted responsibly to avoid negatively impacting the websites being scraped.

- **Rate Limiting:** Implement delays between requests to avoid overwhelming a website's server with traffic.[6] This prevents your scraper from disrupting the website's performance or causing denial-of-service issues.[7]

- **Respectful Scraping:** Only scrape the data you need and avoid unnecessary requests.[8] Excessive scraping can put a strain on server resources and potentially harm the website's operation.[9]
- **Monitoring Impact:** Be mindful of the potential impact of your scraping activities. If you notice any performance issues or errors on the website, adjust your scraping strategy accordingly.

4. Protecting Privacy

When scraping data, it's crucial to be mindful of privacy concerns, especially when dealing with personal information.

- **Personal Data:** Avoid scraping sensitive personal data like names, addresses, email addresses, or phone numbers unless explicitly permitted by the website or required for a legitimate purpose with user consent.[10]
- **Data Security:** Implement appropriate security measures to protect the data you collect, especially if it includes personal information.
- **Compliance with Regulations:** Be aware of and comply with relevant data privacy regulations like GDPR (General Data Protection Regulation) and CCPA (California Consumer Privacy Act).[11]

5. Copyright Considerations

Respect copyright laws when scraping content from websites.

- **Copyright Infringement:** Avoid scraping copyrighted material, such as articles, images, or videos, without permission from the copyright holder.[12]
- **Fair Use:** In some cases, limited use of copyrighted material may be permissible under "fair use" principles, but this is a complex legal area. Consult with legal counsel if you have questions about copyright and web scraping.

By adhering to these legal and ethical guidelines, you can ensure that your web scraping activities are conducted responsibly and sustainably, fostering a positive relationship with the websites you interact with and avoiding potential legal challenges.

Chapter 2: Essential Web Technologies

Understanding HTML: Elements, Attributes, and Structure

Before we can write code to extract data from websites, we need to understand the underlying technologies that make up the web. This chapter focuses on HTML, the foundational language that structures web pages.[1] Mastering HTML is crucial for effective web scraping, as it allows you to identify the data you need within the complex structure of a web page.

Understanding HTML: Elements, Attributes, and Structure

HTML (HyperText Markup Language) is the code that web browsers use to display web pages.[3] It provides a structured way to organize and present content such as text, images, videos, and links.[4] Think of HTML as the skeleton of a web page, defining its layout and the relationships between different elements.[5]

1. HTML Elements

HTML elements are the building blocks of a web page.[6] They are represented by tags enclosed in angle brackets (< >). Most elements have an opening tag (e.g., <p>) and a closing tag (e.g., </p>) with content in between.

- **Examples of HTML elements:**
  - `<h1>` to `<h6>`: Heading elements for different levels of headings.
  - `<p>`: Paragraph element for text content.
  - `<a>`: Anchor element for creating hyperlinks.
  - `<img>`: Image element for displaying images.
  - `<div>`: Division element for grouping and styling sections of content.
  - `<ul>` and `<li>`: Unordered list and list item elements.
  - `<table>`: Table element for creating tables.

2. HTML Attributes

Attributes provide additional information about HTML elements.[7] They are placed within the opening tag of an element and consist of a name-value pair.[8]

- **Examples of HTML attributes:**
  - href (in `<a>` tag): Specifies the URL of a hyperlink.
  - src (in `<img>` tag): Specifies the source of an image.
  - class (in many tags): Assigns a CSS class to an element for styling.
  - id (in many tags): Gives a unique identifier to an element.

- o style (in many tags): Applies inline CSS styles to an element.

3. HTML Structure

HTML documents have a hierarchical structure, often represented as a tree.[9] The basic structure of an HTML document looks like this:

HTML

```
<!DOCTYPE html>

<html>

<head>

 <title>Page Title</title>

 </head>

<body>


 <h1>This is a heading</h1>

 <p>This is a paragraph of text.</p>


</body>

</html>
```

- <!DOCTYPE html>: Declaration that defines the document type and version of HTML.[10]
- <html>: The root element of the HTML document.[11]
- <head>: Contains meta-information about the page, such as the title and character set.[12]
- <title>: Specifies the title that appears in the browser tab.[13]
- <body>: Contains the visible content of the web page.[14]

4. Nesting Elements

HTML elements can be nested within each other to create complex structures and layouts.[15] For example:

HTML

<div class="container">

  <h2>Product Information</h2>

  <p>This is a description of the product.</p>

  <ul>

   <li>Feature 1</li>

   <li>Feature 2</li>

```
</ul>

</div>
```

In this example, the <h2>, <p>, and <ul> elements are nested within the <div> element. This nesting defines the relationships between different content sections.[16]

5. Understanding the DOM (Document Object Model)

When a web browser loads an HTML document, it creates a tree-like representation of the page's structure called the Document Object Model (DOM).[17] The DOM allows JavaScript to interact with and manipulate the elements and content of a web page.[18] Web scraping often involves interacting with the DOM to extract data.[19]

By understanding HTML elements, attributes, and structure, you gain the ability to navigate web pages and pinpoint the data you need for your web scraping projects.[20] In the next section, we'll explore CSS selectors, a powerful tool for targeting specific HTML elements.

CSS Selectors for Targeting Content

CSS selectors are fundamental to web scraping because they provide a precise way to target the specific HTML elements you want to extract data from. Think of them as a query language for HTML. By mastering CSS selectors, you can efficiently pinpoint the elements containing the information you need, even within complex web page structures.

1. Types of CSS Selectors

- **Type Selectors:** Select elements based on their HTML tag name.
    - Example: p selects all paragraph elements.
- **Class Selectors:** Select elements based on their class attribute.
    - Example: .product-title selects all elements with the class "product-title".
- **ID Selectors:** Select a single element based on its id attribute.
    - Example: #price selects the element with the ID "price".
- **Attribute Selectors:** Select elements based on the presence or value of an attribute.
    - Example: [href] selects all elements with an href attribute (typically links).

- Example: [data-price="19.99"] selects elements with a data-price attribute equal to "19.99".
- **Descendant Combinator:** Selects all descendants of an element.
  - Example: div p selects all paragraph elements that are descendants of a <div> element.
- **Child Combinator:** Selects only the direct children of an element.
  - Example: ul > li selects all list items that are direct children of a <ul> element.
- **Adjacent Sibling Combinator:** Selects the element immediately following a specific element.
  - Example: h2 + p selects the paragraph element that immediately follows an <h2> element.
- **General Sibling Combinator:** Selects all elements that are siblings of a specific element and appear after it.
  - Example: h2 ~ p selects all paragraph elements that are siblings of an <h2> element and appear after it.

2. Combining Selectors

You can combine multiple selectors to create more specific and complex targets.

- **Example:** div.product-card h2.title selects <h2> elements with the class "title" that are descendants of <div> elements with the class "product-card".

3. Pseudo-classes

Pseudo-classes allow you to select elements based on their state or position within the document.

- :hover: Selects an element when the user hovers over it.
- :first-child: Selects the first child element of its parent.
- :nth-child(n): Selects the nth child element of its parent.
- :last-child: Selects the last child element of its parent.

4. Using CSS Selectors in Web Scraping

Web scraping libraries like Beautiful Soup often use CSS selectors to locate and extract data from HTML.

- **Example (Beautiful Soup):**

Python

```
from bs4 import BeautifulSoup
```

```python
html = """
<div class="product">
  <h2 class="title">Product Name</h2>
  <p class="price">$19.99</p>
</div>
"""


soup = BeautifulSoup(html, 'html.parser')


# Extract the product title
title = soup.select_one('div.product h2.title').text
print(title)  # Output: Product Name


# Extract the product price
price = soup.select_one('div.product p.price').text
print(price)  # Output: $19.99
```

In this example, select_one finds the first element that matches the CSS selector.

By understanding and effectively using CSS selectors, you can precisely target the data you need within HTML documents, making your web scraping efforts more efficient and accurate. In the next section, we'll explore how to use Python and its libraries to start scraping data from the web.

Basic JavaScript for Dynamic Content

While HTML provides the structure of a web page, JavaScript brings it to life. JavaScript is a programming language that enables dynamic, interactive elements on websites. Understanding the basics of JavaScript is crucial for web scraping, especially when dealing with websites that load content dynamically or rely heavily on JavaScript for functionality.

1. Why JavaScript Matters for Web Scraping

Many modern websites use JavaScript to:

- **Load content asynchronously:** This means content is fetched and displayed without requiring a full page reload. Examples include infinite scrolling, where new content loads as you scroll down, and single-page applications, where content updates dynamically within the same page.

- **Modify the DOM:** JavaScript can change the structure, content, and styling of a web page after it has loaded. This can make it challenging to scrape data if the content you need is generated or manipulated by JavaScript.
- **Handle user interactions:** JavaScript powers interactive elements like buttons, forms, and animations, which can affect the data displayed on a page.

2. Key JavaScript Concepts

- **Variables:** Used to store data values.
    - let name = "John Doe";
- **Data Types:** JavaScript has various data types, including strings ("hello"), numbers (123), booleans (true or false), objects ({ name: "John", age: 30 }), and arrays ([1, 2, 3]).
- **Operators:** Used to perform operations on data, such as arithmetic operations (+, -, *, /), comparison operations (==, !=, >, <), and logical operations (&&, ||, !).
- **Functions:** Blocks of code that can be reused.
    - function greet(name) { console.log("Hello, " + name + "!"); }
- **Control Flow:** Statements like if, else, and for that control the execution of code.

- **DOM Manipulation:** JavaScript can access and modify the Document Object Model (DOM) to change the content and structure of a web page.
    - document.getElementById("myElement").innerHTML = "New content";

3. JavaScript and Web Scraping

When scraping dynamic websites, you might need to:

- **Execute JavaScript:** Use tools like Selenium or Playwright to render JavaScript and access the dynamically generated content.
- **Understand AJAX:** AJAX (Asynchronous JavaScript and XML) allows web pages to update content without reloading. You might need to analyze AJAX requests to understand how data is fetched and displayed.
- **Reverse Engineer JavaScript:** In some cases, you might need to analyze the website's JavaScript code to understand how it generates or manipulates the data you need.

4. Example: Modifying Content with JavaScript

HTML

<!DOCTYPE html>

<html>

```html
<head>
  <title>JavaScript Example</title>
</head>
<body>

  <h1 id="myHeading">Original Heading</h1>

  <script>
    // Get the heading element
    let heading = document.getElementById("myHeading");

    // Change the heading text
    heading.innerHTML = "New Heading";
  </script>

</body>
</html>
```

In this example, the JavaScript code gets the <h1> element with the ID "myHeading" and changes its content to "New Heading".

By grasping these basic JavaScript concepts, you'll be better equipped to handle dynamic websites and extract data that might not be readily available in the initial HTML source code. In the next section, we'll explore how to use browser developer tools to inspect web pages and understand their underlying structure and JavaScript behavior.

Developer Tools for Inspecting Web Pages

Modern web browsers come equipped with powerful developer tools that provide invaluable insights into the structure, content, and behavior of web pages. These tools are essential for web scraping, allowing you to:

- **Examine HTML structure:** See the underlying HTML code of a web page, identify relevant elements, and understand how they are organized.
- **Analyze CSS styles:** Inspect the CSS rules applied to elements to understand their styling and how they are visually presented.

- **Debug JavaScript:** Step through JavaScript code, set breakpoints, and examine variables to understand how dynamic content is generated and manipulated.
- **Monitor network requests:** Track the HTTP requests made by a web page, including AJAX requests, to understand how data is fetched and exchanged with the server.

1. Accessing Developer Tools

Most browsers provide access to developer tools through a similar process:

- **Right-click:** Right-click anywhere on a web page and select "Inspect" or "Inspect Element."
- **Keyboard shortcuts:**
  - Chrome & Edge: Ctrl+Shift+I (Windows) or Cmd+Option+I (Mac)
  - Firefox: Ctrl+Shift+I (Windows) or Cmd+Option+I (Mac)
  - Safari: Right-click and select "Inspect Element," or enable the Develop menu in Safari's preferences and use Option+Cmd+I.

2. Key Features of Developer Tools

- **Elements Panel:**

- View and edit the HTML source code of a web page.
- Inspect individual elements and their attributes.
- See the CSS styles applied to elements.
- **Console Panel:**
  - View JavaScript logs and errors.
  - Execute JavaScript code to interact with the page.
  - Debug JavaScript code by setting breakpoints and stepping through execution.
- **Network Panel:**
  - Monitor all network requests made by the page.
  - Inspect request and response headers, content, and timing information.
  - Filter requests by type (e.g., XHR for AJAX requests).
- **Sources Panel:**
  - View the JavaScript files loaded by the page.
  - Debug JavaScript code within its source files.
- **Application Panel:**
  - Inspect cookies, local storage, and other browser data.

3. Using Developer Tools for Web Scraping

- **Identifying Target Elements:** Use the Elements panel to locate the specific HTML elements that contain the data you want to extract. Inspect their attributes and CSS classes to determine the best way to target them with CSS selectors.
- **Understanding Dynamic Content:** Use the Network and Console panels to analyze AJAX requests and JavaScript code to understand how dynamic content is loaded and updated.
- **Debugging Scraping Logic:** If your scraping code isn't working as expected, use the Console panel to debug JavaScript and the Network panel to inspect HTTP requests.

4. Example: Inspecting a Product Page

Imagine you want to scrape product information from an e-commerce website. Using developer tools, you can:

- **Inspect the product title:** Right-click on the product title and select "Inspect." In the Elements panel, you'll see the HTML element (<h2>, <span>, etc.) and its attributes (e.g., class, id).
- **Find the price:** Similarly, inspect the price element to identify its tag and attributes.
- **Check for dynamic loading:** Use the Network panel to see if product details are loaded via AJAX requests. If so, you'll need to consider

using tools like Selenium or Playwright to render the page fully.

By effectively utilizing developer tools, you can gain a deep understanding of web page structure, content, and behavior, which is crucial for successful web scraping. In the next chapter, we'll start writing Python code to make HTTP requests and extract data from web pages.

Chapter 3: Scraping with Python

Setting Up Your Development Environment

Python is a popular and versatile language for web scraping due to its clear syntax, extensive libraries, and strong community support. This chapter guides you through setting up your Python development environment for web scraping, equipping you with the essential tools to start extracting data from the web.

Setting Up Your Development Environment

A well-organized development environment is crucial for efficient coding and project management. Here's a step-by-step guide to setting up your Python environment for web scraping:

1. Install Python

If you don't have Python installed on your system, download the latest version from the official Python website (python.org). Choose the installer appropriate for your operating system (Windows, macOS, or Linux) and follow the installation instructions.

2. Choose a Code Editor or IDE

A code editor or Integrated Development Environment (IDE) is where you'll write and edit your Python code. Some popular options include:

- **VS Code (Visual Studio Code):** A free, open-source editor with excellent Python support, debugging features, and a vast library of extensions.
- **PyCharm:** A powerful IDE specifically designed for Python development, offering advanced features like code completion, refactoring, and debugging tools.
- **Sublime Text:** A lightweight and fast editor with a customizable interface and good Python support.
- **Atom:** A free, open-source editor developed by GitHub, known for its flexibility and hackability.

Choose an editor that suits your preferences and provides a comfortable coding experience.

3. Install Necessary Packages

Web scraping in Python relies on several powerful libraries. Use pip, the Python package installer, to install these packages:

- requests: This library allows you to send HTTP requests to websites and retrieve their content.

Bash

```
pip install requests
```

- **beautifulsoup4**: Beautiful Soup is a library for parsing HTML and XML documents, making it easy to extract data from web pages.

Bash

```
pip install beautifulsoup4
```

- **lxml**: An optional but recommended library that provides fast and efficient HTML and XML parsing capabilities for Beautiful Soup.

Bash

```
pip install lxml
```

4. Create a Project Directory

Organize your web scraping projects by creating dedicated directories to store your code, data, and other project files. This helps maintain a clean and structured workspace.

5. (Optional) Set Up a Virtual Environment

Virtual environments are isolated Python environments that allow you to manage dependencies for different projects independently. This is particularly useful when working on multiple projects with potentially conflicting package requirements.

- **Create a virtual environment:**

Bash

```
python -m venv my_venv
```

(Replace my_venv with your preferred environment name)

- **Activate the virtual environment:**
  - Windows: my_venv\Scripts\activate
  - macOS/Linux: source my_venv/bin/activate

Once activated, any packages you install using pip will be isolated within that environment.

6. Test Your Setup

To ensure everything is working correctly, create a simple Python script and run it:

Python

```
import requests

from bs4 import BeautifulSoup


# Make a request to a website

response = requests.get('https://www.example.com')


# Parse the HTML content

soup = BeautifulSoup(response.content, 'html.parser')
```

```
# Print the page title

print(soup.title.text)
```

Save this code as a .py file (e.g., test_scrape.py) and run it from your terminal using python test_scrape.py. If you see the page title printed, your environment is set up correctly!

With your development environment ready, you're now equipped to start writing Python code for web scraping. In the next section, we'll explore how to use the requests library to make HTTP requests and retrieve web page content.

Making HTTP Requests with the requests Library

The requests library is a cornerstone of web scraping in Python. It provides a simple and intuitive way to send HTTP requests to websites, retrieve their content, and handle various aspects of web communication.

1. Importing the requests Library

Start by importing the requests library into your Python script:

Python

```python
import requests
```

2. Sending a GET Request

The most common type of HTTP request is the GET request, which is used to retrieve data from a web server. Here's how to send a GET request using requests:

Python

```python
response = requests.get('https://www.example.com')
```

This code sends a GET request to https://www.example.com and stores the[1] server's response in the response variable.

3. Accessing the Response

The response object contains various attributes and methods to access information about the server's response:

- status_code: An integer code indicating the status of the response (e.g., 200 for success, 404 for not found).

Python

```python
print(response.status_code)  # Output: 200
```

- content: The raw bytes of the response content (usually HTML).

Python

```python
print(response.content)       #   Output:   b'<!DOCTYPE html>...'
```

- text: The response content decoded as a string (using the encoding specified in the response headers).

Python

```python
print(response.text)  # Output: '<!DOCTYPE html>...'
```

- headers: A dictionary-like object containing the response headers.

Python

```python
print(response.headers['Content-Type'])     # Output: text/html
```

4. Handling Response Status Codes

It's important to check the status code of the response to ensure the request was successful.

Python

```python
if response.status_code == 200:
    # Request was successful, process the content
    print(response.text)
elif response.status_code == 404:
    # Page not found
```

```
    print("Page not found!")
else:
    # Other error occurred
    print("An error occurred:", response.status_code)
```

5. Passing Parameters in GET Requests

You can pass parameters to a GET request using the params argument:

Python

```
payload = {'q': 'python web scraping', 'page': 2}

response = requests.get('https://www.google.com/search',
params=payload)
```

This code sends a GET request to Google Search with the query "python web scraping" and requests the second page of results. The parameters are appended to the URL as a query string.

6. Other HTTP Methods

While GET is the most common, requests supports other HTTP methods:

- **POST:** Used to submit data to the server (e.g., submitting a form).

Python

```
data = {'username': 'user123', 'password': 'password'}

response = requests.post('https://www.example.com/login', data=data)
```

- **PUT:** Used to update existing resources on the server.
- **DELETE:** Used to delete resources on the server.

7. Advanced Features

requests provides many other features for handling various aspects of web communication:

- **Headers:** Customize request headers (e.g., User-Agent) to simulate different browsers or provide authentication information.
- **Cookies:** Handle cookies to maintain session state.
- **Sessions:** Use sessions to persist parameters and cookies across multiple requests.
- **Timeouts:** Set timeouts to prevent requests from hanging indefinitely.
- **Proxies:** Use proxies to send requests through intermediary servers.

By mastering the requests library, you gain the ability to interact with websites programmatically, retrieve their content, and handle various aspects of web communication, laying the foundation for effective web scraping. In the next section, we'll explore how to use Beautiful Soup to parse HTML content and extract data.

Extracting Data with Beautiful Soup

Beautiful Soup is a powerful Python library designed to make sense of messy HTML and XML data. It provides tools to parse web page content, navigate through its structure, and extract the information you need. This section explores how to use Beautiful Soup to effectively extract data for your web scraping projects.

1. Parsing HTML Content

After fetching HTML content using the requests library, you need to parse it with Beautiful Soup to create a structured object that you can work with.

Python

```python
from bs4 import BeautifulSoup
import requests

# Fetch the web page content
response = requests.get('https://www.example.com')

# Parse the HTML content
soup = BeautifulSoup(response.content, 'html.parser')
```

This code creates a BeautifulSoup object named soup, which represents the parsed HTML structure of the web page. The 'html.parser' argument specifies the parser to use. While Python's built-in HTML parser is sufficient for basic tasks, consider using lxml for faster and more robust parsing:

Python

```python
soup = BeautifulSoup(response.content, 'lxml')
```

2. Navigating the HTML Tree

Beautiful Soup allows you to navigate the parsed HTML using various methods:

- **find()**: Finds the first occurrence of an element that matches the given criteria.

Python

```python
first_paragraph = soup.find('p')  # Finds the first <p> tag
```

- **find_all()**: Finds all occurrences of elements that match the given criteria.

Python

```python
all_paragraphs = soup.find_all('p')  # Finds all <p> tags
```

- select(): Finds elements using CSS selectors (recommended for precise targeting).

Python

```
product_titles = soup.select('h2.product-title')  # Finds all <h2> tags with class "product-title"
```

- **Accessing attributes:** Get the value of an element's attribute.

Python

```
link = soup.find('a')

link_url = link['href']   # Gets the value of the href attribute
```

- **Navigating through children and parents:**

Python

```python
parent_div = soup.find('div', class_='container')

child_paragraphs = parent_div.find_all('p')   # Finds all
<p> tags within the div
```

3. Extracting Text and Data

Once you've located the desired elements, you can extract their text content or specific data:

- text: Gets the text content of an element.

Python

```python
heading = soup.find('h1')

heading_text = heading.text   # Extracts the text of the
<h1> tag
```

- **get_text()**: Similar to text, but provides more options for handling whitespace and separators.

Python

```
paragraph = soup.find('p')

paragraph_text = paragraph.get_text(separator=' ', strip=True)  # Extracts text with spaces and removes extra whitespace
```

- **Extracting data from attributes:**

Python

```
image = soup.find('img')

image_source = image['src']  # Extracts the value of the src attribute
```

4. Example: Extracting Product Information

Python

```python
import requests

from bs4 import BeautifulSoup


# Fetch the web page content

response = requests.get('https://www.example.com/products')


# Parse the HTML content

soup = BeautifulSoup(response.content, 'lxml')


# Find all product divs

products = soup.find_all('div', class_='product')


for product in products:
    # Extract product title
    title = product.find('h2', class_='title').text
```

```
# Extract product price

price = product.find('span', class_='price').text


print(f"Product: {title}, Price: {price}")
```

This example demonstrates how to find all product divs, extract the product title and price from each div, and print the information.

By combining the power of requests to fetch web pages and Beautiful Soup to parse and extract data, you have the essential tools to build effective web scrapers. In the following chapters, we'll explore more advanced techniques, including handling dynamic content, working with APIs, and ensuring ethical scraping practices.

Handling Different Data Formats (HTML, XML, JSON)

While HTML is the most common format you'll encounter when web scraping, websites often utilize other data formats like XML and JSON to structure and transmit information. This section explores these formats and how to work with them effectively in your Python web scraping projects.

1. HTML (HyperText Markup Language)

As we've discussed, HTML is the foundation of web pages, using tags to structure content. We use libraries like Beautiful Soup to parse HTML and extract data based on tags and attributes.

Example:

HTML

```
<div class="product">

  <h2 class="title">Product Name</h2>

  <p class="price">$19.99</p>

</div>
```

2. XML (Extensible Markup Language)

XML is a markup language similar to HTML, but it's designed for more general data storage and exchange. XML uses tags to define elements and attributes to provide additional information.

Example:

XML

```
<product>
  <name>Product Name</name>
  <price currency="USD">19.99</price>
</product>
```

Working with XML in Python:

- Use the xml.etree.ElementTree library (built-in) or lxml for more advanced features.

Python

```python
import xml.etree.ElementTree as ET


# Parse the XML string
root = ET.fromstring(xml_string)


# Access elements and attributes
name = root.find('name').text
```

```python
price = root.find('price').text

currency = root.find('price').get('currency')


print(f"Product: {name}, Price: {price} {currency}")
```

3. JSON (JavaScript Object Notation)

JSON is a lightweight data format that is widely used for data exchange, particularly in web APIs. It uses a human-readable format based on key-value pairs and arrays.

Example:

JSON

```json
{

  "name": "Product Name",

  "price": 19.99,

  "currency": "USD"

}
```

Working with JSON in Python:

- Use the json library (built-in) to work with JSON data.

Python

```
import json

# Parse the JSON string
data = json.loads(json_string)

# Access data using keys
name = data['name']
price = data['price']
currency = data['currency']

print(f"Product: {name}, Price: {price} {currency}")
```

4. Choosing the Right Tool

- **Beautiful Soup:** Primarily for HTML and XML parsing, especially when dealing with irregular or poorly formatted markup.
- xml.etree.ElementTree: Suitable for well-formed XML documents.
- lxml: A faster and more feature-rich library for both HTML and XML processing.
- json: The standard library for handling JSON data in Python.

5. Example: Handling Different Formats in a Scraper

Python

```python
import requests

from bs4 import BeautifulSoup

import json


# ... (code to fetch web page content) ...


if 'Content-Type' in response.headers:

    content_type = response.headers['Content-Type']


    if 'html' in content_type:
```

```python
        # Parse HTML with Beautiful Soup

        soup = BeautifulSoup(response.content, 'lxml')

        # ... (extract data from HTML) ...

    elif 'xml' in content_type:

        # Parse XML with xml.etree.ElementTree

        # ... (extract data from XML) ...

    elif 'json' in content_type:

        # Parse JSON with json library

        data = json.loads(response.content)

        # ... (extract data from JSON) ...
```

This example demonstrates how to check the Content-Type header of the response to determine the data format and use the appropriate library for parsing.

By understanding and being able to handle different data formats, you become a more versatile web scraper, capable of extracting information from a wider range of websites and APIs. In the next chapter, we'll move beyond basic scraping and explore how to handle websites that load content dynamically using JavaScript.

Part II: Concurrent Web Scraping in Python

Chapter 4: Introduction to Concurrency

Why Concurrency Matters for Web Scraping

Web scraping often involves fetching data from multiple pages, sometimes even hundreds or thousands. Imagine a scenario where you need to extract product information from an online store with over 10,000 items. Fetching each page sequentially, one after the other, would be incredibly time-consuming. This is where concurrency comes to the rescue.

Why Concurrency Matters for Web Scraping

Concurrency is the ability of a program to execute multiple tasks seemingly at the same time. In the context of web scraping, it means fetching multiple web pages concurrently, rather than waiting for each request to complete before sending the next one. This significantly speeds up the scraping process and improves efficiency.

1. The Limitations of Sequential Scraping

In sequential scraping, each request is handled one at a time:

1. Send request to website.
2. Wait for the server to respond.
3. Process the response (extract data).
4. Repeat for the next request.

This approach introduces significant latency, especially when dealing with many requests. Much of the time is spent waiting for the server to respond, while your program remains idle.

2. The Benefits of Concurrent Scraping

Concurrent scraping overcomes these limitations by allowing multiple requests to be processed simultaneously:

1. Send multiple requests to the website concurrently.
2. As responses arrive, process them without waiting for others.

This dramatically reduces the overall scraping time by utilizing the waiting time more effectively.

Key Advantages of Concurrency:

- **Increased Speed:** Fetching multiple pages concurrently significantly reduces the total time required for scraping.
- **Improved Efficiency:** Utilizes system resources more effectively by avoiding idle time.
- **Enhanced Responsiveness:** Your program remains responsive while waiting for responses, allowing you to perform other tasks or handle user interactions.

- **Scalability:** Concurrent scrapers can handle a larger number of requests and scale more effectively to handle growing data needs.

3. Concurrency vs. Parallelism

While often used interchangeably, concurrency and parallelism have distinct meanings:

- **Concurrency:** Managing multiple tasks at the same time. This can be achieved even on a single-core processor by switching between tasks rapidly.
- **Parallelism:** Executing multiple tasks truly simultaneously, requiring multiple cores or processors.

Concurrency is a more general concept, while parallelism is a specific form of concurrency that requires hardware support. In Python, concurrency can be achieved through techniques like threading and asynchronous programming.

4. Use Cases for Concurrency in Web Scraping

- **Large-scale scraping:** When scraping thousands of pages or websites, concurrency is essential to complete the task in a reasonable time.
- **Real-time data extraction:** For applications that require up-to-date data, concurrency allows you

to fetch and process information from multiple sources concurrently.

- **Scraping data from APIs:** Many APIs have rate limits, and concurrency can help you stay within those limits while maximizing data extraction.

By understanding the importance of concurrency and its benefits for web scraping, you can build more efficient, scalable, and robust scrapers that can handle even the most demanding data extraction tasks. In the next section, we'll explore the concepts of threads and processes, which are fundamental to implementing concurrency in Python.

Threads and Processes: A Comparison

In Python, concurrency can be achieved using threads or processes. Both allow you to execute multiple tasks seemingly simultaneously, but they differ in how they utilize system resources and interact with each other. Understanding these differences is crucial for choosing the right approach for your web scraping needs.

1. Processes

- **Independent Execution:** Processes are independent instances of a program with their own memory space. This means they don't share data directly and are isolated from each other.

- **Resource Intensive:** Each process has its own overhead in terms of memory and system resources. Creating and managing processes can be more resource-intensive than threads.
- **Robustness:** If one process crashes, it generally doesn't affect other processes running on the system.
- **Inter-process Communication:** Communication between processes requires explicit mechanisms like pipes or message queues.

2. Threads

- **Shared Memory:** Threads exist within a single process and share the same memory space. This allows for easier data sharing between threads.
- **Lightweight:** Threads have lower overhead than processes, making them more efficient in terms of resource usage.
- **Concurrency, Not Parallelism:** In CPython (the standard Python implementation), due to the Global Interpreter Lock (GIL), only one thread can execute Python bytecode at a time. This means threads achieve concurrency but not true parallelism for CPU-bound tasks.
- **Synchronization Challenges:** Sharing memory introduces the need for synchronization mechanisms (e.g., locks, semaphores) to prevent race conditions and ensure data consistency.

3. Comparison Table

Feature	Processes	Threads
Memory space	Separate	Shared
Resource usage	Higher	Lower
Isolation	High	Low
Communication	More complex	Easier
True parallelism (CPython)	Yes	No (due to GIL)
Robustness	Higher	Lower

4. Choosing Between Threads and Processes

- **CPU-bound tasks:** If your scraping tasks involve heavy computation (e.g., data processing, image analysis), processes are generally preferred as they can utilize multiple CPU cores for true parallelism.
- **I/O-bound tasks:** For tasks that involve a lot of waiting for network requests (which is often the case in web scraping), threads can be more efficient due to their lower overhead.

- **Data sharing:** If your tasks require frequent data sharing, threads provide a simpler mechanism due to shared memory.
- **Complexity:** Threads can introduce complexities related to synchronization and potential race conditions. Processes offer better isolation and robustness.

5. Example: Threads vs. Processes for Web Scraping

- **Threads:** Suitable for scraping multiple pages from the same website concurrently, as they can share session data and cookies easily.
- **Processes:** Might be preferred when scraping data from different websites or APIs with varying requirements, as they provide better isolation and fault tolerance.

By understanding the characteristics of threads and processes, you can make informed decisions about which approach is best suited for your specific web scraping needs. In the next section, we will explore how to implement concurrency in Python using the concurrent.futures module.

Asynchronous Programming with asyncio

Asynchronous programming is a powerful paradigm that allows you to write concurrent code that appears to execute multiple tasks simultaneously, even with a single thread. In Python, the asyncio library provides a framework for writing asynchronous code, making it particularly well-suited for I/O-bound tasks like web scraping.

1. The asyncio Event Loop

At the heart of asyncio is the event loop. The event loop is a single-threaded process that manages and runs asynchronous tasks. It continuously monitors tasks, allowing them to run when they are ready and suspending them when they are waiting for I/O operations (like network requests), effectively utilizing the waiting time to execute other tasks.

2. Coroutines and async/await

Coroutines are special functions defined using the async keyword. They can pause their execution using the await keyword, allowing other coroutines to run while they are waiting for I/O. This "cooperative multitasking" is the key to achieving concurrency with asyncio.

Example:

Python

```
import asyncio
```

```python
async def fetch_data(url):
    # Simulate an I/O-bound operation (e.g., network request)
    await asyncio.sleep(1)  # Wait for 1 second
    return f"Data from {url}"


async def main():
    # Create tasks for fetching data from multiple URLs
    tasks = [fetch_data("url1"), fetch_data("url2"), fetch_data("url3")]

    # Gather the results of the tasks
    results = await asyncio.gather(*tasks)

    # Print the results
    for result in results:
        print(result)
```

```
# Run the main coroutine in the event loop

asyncio.run(main())
```

In this example, fetch_data is a coroutine that simulates fetching data from a URL. The main coroutine creates tasks for fetching data from multiple URLs and uses asyncio.gather to run them concurrently.

3. Benefits of asyncio for Web Scraping

- **Efficiency:** asyncio excels at handling I/O-bound tasks like web scraping, efficiently utilizing waiting time for other tasks.
- **Single-threaded Concurrency:** Achieves concurrency without the overhead of managing multiple threads.
- **Improved Responsiveness:** The event loop ensures that your program remains responsive while waiting for network requests.
- **Scalability:** Can handle a large number of concurrent connections effectively.

4. When to Use asyncio

- **I/O-bound tasks:** asyncio is ideal for web scraping, as it efficiently handles the waiting time involved in network requests.

- **High concurrency:** When you need to handle many concurrent connections or requests.
- **Asynchronous libraries:** Many libraries are now providing asyncio-compatible versions, making it easier to integrate asynchronous programming into your projects.

5. Considerations

- **Learning curve:** asyncio can have a steeper learning curve compared to traditional threading.
- **Blocking operations:** Avoid using blocking operations within coroutines, as they can stall the event loop and hinder concurrency.
- **Debugging:** Debugging asynchronous code can be more challenging, requiring specialized tools and techniques.

By understanding the principles of asynchronous programming with asyncio, you can unlock a powerful approach to concurrent web scraping, enabling you to build highly efficient and scalable scrapers that can handle a large number of requests with ease. In the next chapter, we'll put these concepts into practice and build a concurrent web scraper using concurrent.futures.

Chapter 5: Concurrency in Action

Building a Concurrent Web Scraper with concurrent.futures

Building upon our understanding of concurrency, this chapter demonstrates how to implement a concurrent web scraper in Python using the concurrent.futures module. This module provides a high-level interface for asynchronously executing callables (functions or methods) using either threads or processes, making it a versatile tool for concurrent web scraping.

Building a Concurrent Web Scraper with concurrent.futures

The concurrent.futures module offers two primary classes for concurrent execution:

- ThreadPoolExecutor: Uses a pool of threads to execute tasks concurrently.
- ProcessPoolExecutor: Uses a pool of processes to execute tasks concurrently.

We'll focus on ThreadPoolExecutor for this example, as it's generally well-suited for I/O-bound tasks like web scraping.

1. Import necessary modules

Python

```
import requests

from bs4 import BeautifulSoup

from concurrent.futures import ThreadPoolExecutor,
as_completed
```

2. Define the scraping function

Create a function that takes a URL as input, fetches the web page content, and extracts the desired data.

Python

```
def scrape_page(url):
    response = requests.get(url)
    soup = BeautifulSoup(response.content, 'lxml')


    # Extract data (replace with your specific logic)
    title = soup.find('h1').text
    return title
```

3. Create a list of URLs

Prepare a list of URLs that you want to scrape.

Python

```python
urls = [
    "https://www.example.com/page1",
    "https://www.example.com/page2",
    "https://www.example.com/page3",
    # ... more URLs
]
```

4. Use ThreadPoolExecutor **to scrape concurrently**

Create a ThreadPoolExecutor and use its submit()
method to schedule the scrape_page function for each
URL.

Python

```python
with ThreadPoolExecutor(max_workers=5) as executor:
    # Submit tasks to the executor
```

```
    futures = [executor.submit(scrape_page, url) for url in
urls]


    # Process the results as they become available

    for future in as_completed(futures):
        try:
            title = future.result()  # Get the result of the task
            print(f"Extracted title: {title}")
        except Exception as e:
            print(f"Error scraping URL: {e}")
```

This code creates a thread pool with a maximum of 5
worker threads. It then submits tasks to the executor,
each task responsible for scraping a single URL. The
as_completed function provides an iterator that yields
futures as they complete, allowing you to process results
as they become available.

5. Key Considerations

- max_workers: This parameter controls the
  maximum number of threads in the pool. Choose
  a value that balances resource usage and scraping

speed. A good starting point is often the number of CPU cores or slightly higher.

- **Error handling:** Include error handling (using try-except blocks) to gracefully handle potential exceptions during scraping.
- **Rate limiting:** If the website has rate limits, adjust your code to introduce delays or use other techniques to avoid exceeding the limits.
- **Synchronization:** If your scraping tasks need to share data or resources, use appropriate synchronization mechanisms (e.g., locks) to ensure data consistency.

6. Benefits of concurrent.futures

- **Simplified concurrency:** Provides a high-level interface for managing threads or processes, making it easier to implement concurrency.
- **Flexibility:** Allows you to choose between threads or processes based on your needs.
- **Improved performance:** Significantly speeds up web scraping by executing tasks concurrently.

By utilizing concurrent.futures, you can effectively implement concurrency in your web scraping projects, leading to faster, more efficient, and more robust data extraction. In the next chapter, we'll explore asynchronous scraping using the asyncio library, providing another powerful approach to concurrency.

Using Thread Pools and Process Pools

The concurrent.futures module provides two primary classes for creating pools of workers: ThreadPoolExecutor and ProcessPoolExecutor. These pools allow you to manage and reuse workers (threads or processes) to execute multiple tasks concurrently, improving efficiency and resource utilization.

1. Thread Pools (ThreadPoolExecutor)

Thread pools are suitable for I/O-bound tasks, like web scraping, where tasks spend a significant amount of time waiting for network requests.

- **Creating a thread pool:**

Python

```
from concurrent.futures import ThreadPoolExecutor


with ThreadPoolExecutor(max_workers=5) as executor:
    # Submit tasks to the executor
    # ...
```

This creates a thread pool with a maximum of 5 worker threads. The with statement ensures that the pool is properly shut down after its use.

- **Submitting tasks:**

Python

future = executor.submit(scrape_page, url)

This submits the scrape_page function with the given URL to the executor, scheduling it for execution in a separate thread.

- **Retrieving results:**

Python

title = future.result()

This retrieves the result of the task once it's completed. The result() method will block until the result is available.

2. Process Pools (ProcessPoolExecutor)

Process pools are generally preferred for CPU-bound tasks, where tasks involve heavy computation and can benefit from true parallelism across multiple CPU cores.

- **Creating a process pool:**

Python

```python
from concurrent.futures import ProcessPoolExecutor

with ProcessPoolExecutor(max_workers=4) as executor:
    # Submit tasks to the executor
    # ...
```

This creates a process pool with a maximum of 4 worker processes.

- **Submitting and retrieving results:** The methods for submitting tasks and retrieving results are the same as with ThreadPoolExecutor.

3. Choosing the Right Pool

- **I/O-bound tasks (web scraping):** ThreadPoolExecutor is often more efficient due to lower overhead.
- **CPU-bound tasks (data processing):** ProcessPoolExecutor can utilize multiple cores for true parallelism.
- **Data sharing:** Thread pools allow easier data sharing due to shared memory, but require careful synchronization.
- **Overhead:** Process pools have higher overhead due to process creation and inter-process communication.

4. Example: Using Process Pools for Data Processing

Python

```python
from concurrent.futures import ProcessPoolExecutor


def process_data(data):
    # Perform CPU-intensive processing on the data
    # ...
    return processed_data


with ProcessPoolExecutor() as executor:
```

```python
# Submit data processing tasks

futures = [executor.submit(process_data, item) for item in data_list]


# Retrieve the processed results

for future in as_completed(futures):

    processed_item = future.result()

    # ...
```

This example demonstrates how to use a process pool to perform CPU-intensive data processing tasks concurrently.

By understanding how to use thread pools and process pools effectively, you can optimize your web scraping projects for both I/O-bound and CPU-bound operations, leading to significant performance improvements. In the next chapter, we'll explore asynchronous scraping with asyncio, providing another powerful approach to concurrency.

Managing Resources and Avoiding Race Conditions

When working with concurrent code, especially with threads that share memory, it's crucial to manage resources carefully and prevent race conditions. Race conditions occur when multiple threads access and modify shared data simultaneously, leading to unpredictable and potentially erroneous behavior. This section outlines strategies for managing resources and avoiding race conditions in your concurrent web scraping projects.

1. Understanding Race Conditions

Imagine two threads scraping product information and updating a shared dictionary to store the data. If both threads try to modify the same key in the dictionary simultaneously, one thread's changes might overwrite the other's, leading to data loss or inconsistency. This is a classic example of a race condition.

2. Synchronization Primitives

Python provides synchronization primitives to control access to shared resources and prevent race conditions:

- **Locks:** A lock allows only one thread to acquire it at a time. Other threads must wait until the lock is released.

Python

```python
import threading

# Create a lock
lock = threading.Lock()

# Acquire the lock before accessing shared data
lock.acquire()
try:
    # Access and modify shared data
    # ...
finally:
    # Always release the lock
    lock.release()
```

- **Semaphores:** A semaphore allows a limited number of threads to access a resource concurrently.
- **Conditions:** A condition allows threads to wait for a specific condition to become true before proceeding.
- **Queues:** Queues provide a thread-safe way to exchange data between threads.

3. Strategies for Avoiding Race Conditions

- **Minimize shared state:** Reduce the amount of shared data between threads as much as possible. Design your code to keep data local to each thread whenever feasible.
- **Use thread-safe data structures:** If you need to share data, use thread-safe data structures like queues or concurrent dictionaries.
- **Apply locks strategically:** Use locks to protect critical sections of code where shared data is accessed and modified. Acquire the lock before accessing the data and release it afterward.
- **Choose the right granularity:** Balance the use of locks to avoid excessive locking, which can hinder concurrency, and too little locking, which can lead to race conditions.
- **Consider alternative concurrency models:** If managing shared state becomes too complex,

explore alternative models like asynchronous programming with asyncio, which avoids shared state by design.

4. Example: Using a Lock to Protect Shared Data

Python

```python
import threading


# Shared data
data_dict = {}
lock = threading.Lock()


def scrape_and_store(url):
    # ... (scrape data from the URL) ...


    # Acquire the lock before updating the dictionary
    with lock:
        data_dict[url] = scraped_data
```

```python
# Create and start threads
threads = []
for url in urls:
    thread = threading.Thread(target=scrape_and_store, args=(url,))
    threads.append(thread)
    thread.start()


# Wait for threads to finish
for thread in threads:
    thread.join()
```

In this example, a lock is used to protect the shared data_dict dictionary, ensuring that only one thread can update it at a time.

By carefully managing resources and applying appropriate synchronization techniques, you can prevent race conditions and ensure the reliability and correctness of your concurrent web scraping code. In the next chapter, we'll explore asynchronous scraping with asyncio, which offers an alternative approach to

concurrency with its own set of benefits and
considerations.

Chapter 6: Asynchronous Scraping

Mastering asyncio for High-Performance Scraping

Asynchronous programming, using the asyncio library, offers a powerful approach to concurrent web scraping in Python. This chapter explores how to master asyncio to build high-performance scrapers that efficiently handle a large number of requests and maximize data extraction speed.

Mastering asyncio for High-Performance Scraping

asyncio leverages an event loop to manage and run asynchronous tasks, enabling concurrency within a single thread. By understanding the core concepts of asyncio and applying best practices, you can significantly enhance the performance of your web scrapers.

1. Essential asyncio Concepts

- **Event Loop:** The event loop is the core of asyncio. It's a single-threaded process that monitors and runs asynchronous tasks, allowing them to execute concurrently.
- **Coroutines:** Coroutines are special functions defined using the async keyword. They can pause

their execution using await, enabling other coroutines to run while they wait for I/O operations.

- **Tasks:** Tasks represent units of work scheduled to run on the event loop. They are created from coroutines using asyncio.create_task().
- async/await **Syntax:** The async keyword defines a coroutine, and await is used to pause a coroutine's execution until an awaited coroutine completes.

2. Building an Asynchronous Scraper

Here's a basic example of an asynchronous web scraper using asyncio and the aiohttp library (an asynchronous HTTP client):

Python

```python
import asyncio

import aiohttp

from bs4 import BeautifulSoup


async def fetch_page(session, url):

    async with session.get(url) as response:

        return await response.text()
```

```python
async def scrape_page(url):
    async with aiohttp.ClientSession() as session:
        html = await fetch_page(session, url)
        soup = BeautifulSoup(html, 'lxml')
        # Extract data from soup
        # ...
        return extracted_data


async def main():
    urls = [
        "https://www.example.com/page1",
        "https://www.example.com/page2",
        # ... more URLs
    ]
    tasks = [asyncio.create_task(scrape_page(url)) for url in urls]
    results = await asyncio.gather(*tasks)
```

```
    # Process the results
    # ...


asyncio.run(main())
```

This code defines coroutines for fetching web pages (fetch_page) and scraping data (scrape_page). The main coroutine creates tasks for each URL and uses asyncio.gather to run them concurrently.

3. Optimizing for Performance

- **Efficient HTTP Requests:** Use an asynchronous HTTP client like aiohttp to make non-blocking requests.
- **Connection Pooling:** Reuse connections to the same server to reduce overhead. aiohttp provides built-in connection pooling.
- **Limit Concurrency:** While asyncio can handle many concurrent tasks, setting a reasonable limit (e.g., using asyncio.Semaphore) can prevent overloading the server or your system.
- **Avoid Blocking Operations:** Ensure that your coroutines don't perform blocking operations (e.g., long-running calculations, synchronous file I/O) that can stall the event loop.

4. Handling Errors and Timeouts

- try-except **Blocks:** Wrap your coroutines in try-except blocks to handle potential exceptions, including aiohttp.ClientError for network errors and asyncio.TimeoutError for timeouts.
- **Timeouts:** Set timeouts for requests to prevent your scraper from hanging indefinitely. aiohttp allows you to set timeouts for individual requests or for the entire session.

5. Advanced Techniques

- **Asynchronous Context Managers:** Use async with to manage resources like HTTP sessions and ensure proper cleanup.
- **Task Cancellation:** Cancel tasks that are no longer needed or taking too long to complete.
- **Custom Event Loops:** For advanced use cases, you can create and customize your own event loops.

By mastering asyncio and applying these optimization techniques, you can build high-performance web scrapers that efficiently extract data from multiple sources concurrently. In the next chapter, we'll move beyond basic scraping and explore techniques for scraping dynamic websites that rely heavily on JavaScript.

Working with Asynchronous HTTP Requests

Asynchronous HTTP requests are the foundation of efficient asynchronous web scraping. By utilizing libraries like aiohttp, you can send multiple requests concurrently without blocking the execution of other tasks. This section explores how to effectively work with asynchronous HTTP requests in your asyncio-powered scrapers.

1. Introducing aiohttp

aiohttp is a popular asynchronous HTTP client/server framework for Python. It provides an API for making asynchronous HTTP requests and handling responses within the asyncio event loop.

Installation:

Bash

```
pip install aiohttp
```

2. Making Asynchronous GET Requests

Python

```
import aiohttp
```

```python
import asyncio

async def fetch_page(url):
    async with aiohttp.ClientSession() as session:
        async with session.get(url) as response:
            # Check the response status
            if response.status == 200:
                html = await response.text()
                return html
            else:
                print(f"Error fetching {url}: {response.status}")
                return None

async def main():
    url = "https://www.example.com"
    html = await fetch_page(url)
    if html:
```

```
    # Process the HTML content

    print(html[:100])  # Print the first 100 characters


asyncio.run(main())
```

This code defines a fetch_page coroutine that creates an aiohttp.ClientSession and uses it to send an asynchronous GET request to the specified URL. The async with statement ensures proper resource cleanup.

3. Handling Responses

The response object provides various methods to access information about the response:

- status: The HTTP status code of the response (e.g., 200 for success, 404 for not found).
- text(): Asynchronously reads the response body as text.
- json(): Asynchronously reads the response body as JSON.
- headers: A dictionary-like object containing the response headers.

4. POST Requests and Sending Data

Python

```python
async def submit_form(url, data):
    async with aiohttp.ClientSession() as session:
        async with session.post(url, data=data) as response:
            # ... handle the response ...
```

Use the post() method to send a POST request. The data argument can be a dictionary, a string, or a file-like object.

5. Headers and Cookies

You can customize request headers and handle cookies using the headers and cookies arguments in the get() or post() methods.

Python

```python
headers = {'User-Agent': 'My Custom User Agent'}
cookies = {'session_id': '12345'}


async with session.get(url, headers=headers, cookies=cookies) as response:
```

6. Connection Pooling

aiohttp provides built-in connection pooling, which reuses connections to the same server, reducing overhead and improving performance. You can configure the connection pool using the connector argument when creating a ClientSession.

7. Error Handling

Wrap your asynchronous HTTP requests in try-except blocks to handle potential exceptions like aiohttp.ClientError (for network errors) and asyncio.TimeoutError (for timeouts).

By effectively utilizing aiohttp and understanding how to work with asynchronous HTTP requests, you can build highly efficient web scrapers that can handle a large number of requests concurrently without blocking the event loop. In the next section, we'll explore how to build a complete asynchronous web scraper.

Building an Asynchronous Web Scraper

Now that we've explored the essential components of asynchronous scraping with asyncio and aiohttp, let's put them together to build a complete asynchronous web scraper. This example demonstrates how to fetch multiple web pages concurrently, extract data from them, and process the results efficiently.

1. Define the Target Website and Data

For this example, let's assume we want to scrape product information (title, price, and description) from an e-commerce website. We'll use a simplified HTML structure for demonstration:

HTML

```
<div class="product">
  <h2 class="title">Product Name</h2>
  <p class="price">$19.99</p>
  <div class="description">Product description...</div>
</div>
```

2. Import Necessary Libraries

Python

```
import asyncio
```

```python
import aiohttp

from bs4 import BeautifulSoup
```

3. Create the fetch_page Coroutine

This coroutine fetches the HTML content of a given URL using aiohttp:

Python

```python
async def fetch_page(session, url):
    async with session.get(url) as response:
        if response.status == 200:
            return await response.text()
        else:
            print(f"Error fetching {url}: {response.status}")
            return None
```

4. Create the scrape_page Coroutine

This coroutine extracts product information from the HTML content using Beautiful Soup:

```python
Python
async def scrape_page(url):
    async with aiohttp.ClientSession() as session:
        html = await fetch_page(session, url)
        if html:
            soup = BeautifulSoup(html, 'lxml')
            product = soup.find('div', class_='product')
            if product:
                title = product.find('h2', class_='title').text.strip()
                price = product.find('p', class_='price').text.strip()
                description = product.find('div', class_='description').text.strip()
                return {
                    'url': url,
                    'title': title,
                    'price': price,
                    'description': description
```

```python
        }
    else:

        print(f"Product not found on {url}")

        return None
else:

    return None
```

5. Create the main Coroutine

This coroutine defines the list of URLs to scrape, creates tasks for each URL, and gathers the results:

Python

```python
async def main():
    urls = [
        "https://www.example.com/product1",
        "https://www.example.com/product2",
        "https://www.example.com/product3",
        # ... more URLs
    ]
```

```python
    tasks = [asyncio.create_task(scrape_page(url)) for url
in urls]

    results = await asyncio.gather(*tasks)


    # Process the results

    for result in results:

        if result:

            print(f"URL: {result['url']}")

            print(f"Title: {result['title']}")

            print(f"Price: {result['price']}")

            print(f"Description: {result['description']}")

            print("-" * 20)


asyncio.run(main())
```

6. Run the Scraper

Execute the script, and it will asynchronously scrape the specified URLs, extract product information, and print the results.

7. Key Improvements

- **Concurrency:** The scraper fetches multiple pages concurrently, significantly reducing scraping time.
- **Efficiency:** asyncio and aiohttp efficiently handle I/O-bound operations, maximizing resource utilization.
- **Error Handling:** The code includes basic error handling to gracefully handle potential issues during fetching or scraping.

This example provides a solid foundation for building more complex asynchronous web scrapers. You can extend it to handle various data formats, implement more sophisticated data extraction logic, and incorporate features like error handling, logging, and data storage.

Part III: Advanced Scraping Techniques

Chapter 7: Scraping Dynamic Websites

Introduction to JavaScript Rendering

As we venture deeper into the world of web scraping, we encounter websites that are no longer static pages of HTML, but dynamic, interactive experiences powered by JavaScript. This chapter explores the challenges and solutions associated with scraping these dynamic websites, starting with an introduction to JavaScript rendering.

Introduction to JavaScript Rendering

Traditional web scraping techniques, using libraries like requests and Beautiful Soup, excel at extracting data from static HTML content. However, they fall short when dealing with websites that rely heavily on JavaScript to generate or modify content after the initial page load.

1. The Rise of Dynamic Websites

Modern web development trends favor dynamic, interactive user interfaces. JavaScript plays a crucial role in creating these experiences:

- **Single-Page Applications (SPAs):** SPAs load a single HTML page and dynamically update content using JavaScript, providing a seamless user experience.

- **Asynchronous Content Loading:** Content is fetched and displayed on demand without requiring full page reloads, improving performance and interactivity.
- **User Interaction and Data Manipulation:** JavaScript handles user interactions, form submissions, and dynamic content updates, making the web more engaging.

2. Challenges for Web Scraping

These dynamic elements pose challenges for traditional scraping techniques:

- **Hidden Content:** The data you need might not be present in the initial HTML source code. It might be generated or loaded later by JavaScript.
- **JavaScript Execution:** requests only fetches the initial HTML. It doesn't execute JavaScript, so dynamic content remains hidden.
- **API Calls:** Websites often use JavaScript to make API calls to fetch data from the server. These calls are not visible in the initial HTML.

3. Understanding JavaScript Rendering

JavaScript rendering is the process of executing JavaScript code within a web page to generate the final, rendered content that users see in their browsers. This process involves:

- **Parsing HTML:** The browser parses the HTML source code.
- **Fetching Resources:** The browser fetches external resources like CSS and JavaScript files.
- **Executing JavaScript:** The browser executes the JavaScript code, which may:
  - Modify the DOM (Document Object Model), adding, removing, or changing elements.
  - Fetch data from APIs and update the page dynamically.
  - Handle user interactions and events.

4. Why JavaScript Rendering Matters

To effectively scrape dynamic websites, you need a way to simulate this JavaScript rendering process. This allows you to:

- **Access Dynamic Content:** Retrieve data that is generated or loaded by JavaScript after the initial page load.
- **Interact with the Page:** Simulate user interactions like clicking buttons or filling out forms to access content that requires user actions.

- **Capture API Calls:** Intercept and analyze API calls made by JavaScript to understand how data is fetched and potentially access it directly.

In the following sections, we'll explore tools and techniques for performing JavaScript rendering and overcoming the challenges of scraping dynamic websites. We'll examine how to use browser automation tools like Selenium and Playwright to control a headless browser and render JavaScript, enabling us to access the full content of dynamic web pages.

Automating Browsers with Selenium

Selenium is a powerful tool for automating web browsers. It allows you to control a browser programmatically, simulating user interactions like clicking links, filling out forms, and navigating pages. This makes it particularly useful for web scraping dynamic websites that rely on JavaScript.

1. How Selenium Works

Selenium WebDriver is the core component of Selenium that interacts with web browsers. It provides a consistent API for controlling different browsers, including Chrome, Firefox, Edge, and Safari.

- **WebDriver:** Acts as a bridge between your code and the browser, translating your commands into browser-specific actions.
- **Browser Driver:** A separate executable specific to each browser that WebDriver communicates with to control the browser.

2. Setting Up Selenium

- **Install the Selenium library:**

Bash

```
pip install selenium
```

- **Download the browser driver:** Download the appropriate driver for your chosen browser from the Selenium website (selenium.dev/documentation/webdriver/getting_started/install_drivers/).
- **Configure the driver:** In your Python code, specify the path to the downloaded driver executable.

3. Basic Selenium Actions

Python

```python
from selenium import webdriver

from selenium.webdriver.common.by import By


# Configure the browser driver (replace with your driver
path)

driver                                                    =
webdriver.Chrome(executable_path='/path/to/chromedri
ver')


# Navigate to a URL

driver.get("https://www.example.com")


# Find an element by ID

element = driver.find_element(By.ID, "myElement")


# Click the element

element.click()
```

```python
# Find an element by CSS selector
search_box = driver.find_element(By.CSS_SELECTOR,
"input[name='q']")

# Enter text into the search box
search_box.send_keys("Selenium web scraping")

# Submit the form
search_box.submit()

# Get the page title
title = driver.title
print(title)

# Close the browser
driver.quit()
```

This code demonstrates basic actions like navigating to a URL, finding elements, clicking buttons, entering text, and submitting forms.

4. Scraping Dynamic Content

Selenium allows you to wait for JavaScript to render content before extracting it. You can use explicit waits to wait for specific conditions, such as an element to become visible or clickable.

Python

```
from selenium.webdriver.support.ui import WebDriverWait

from selenium.webdriver.support import expected_conditions as EC


# Wait for an element to be clickable

element = WebDriverWait(driver, 10).until(

    EC.element_to_be_clickable((By.ID, "myButton"))

)


# Extract data after JavaScript rendering
```

```
data      =      driver.find_element(By.CSS_SELECTOR,
"div.content").text
```

5. Headless Browsing

For web scraping, you often don't need to see the browser visually. You can run Selenium in headless mode, where the browser operates in the background without a graphical user interface.

Python

```
options = webdriver.ChromeOptions()

options.add_argument('--headless')

driver = webdriver.Chrome(options=options)
```

6. Best Practices

- **Explicit Waits:** Use explicit waits to ensure that elements are loaded and interactable before performing actions.
- **Efficient Locators:** Use efficient locators (IDs, CSS selectors) to find elements quickly.
- **Headless Mode:** Run Selenium in headless mode for faster scraping and reduced resource usage.

- **Respect Website Terms:** Adhere to website terms of service and robots.txt to avoid being blocked.

By utilizing Selenium's capabilities, you can effectively scrape dynamic websites, access content rendered by JavaScript, and interact with web pages programmatically. In the next section, we'll explore another powerful browser automation tool, Playwright, which offers similar functionalities with some distinct advantages.

Headless Browsing with Playwright

Playwright is a powerful Node.js library developed by Microsoft for automating web browsers. It offers similar functionalities to Selenium but with some key advantages, including broader browser support (Chromium, Firefox, and WebKit), improved performance, and a more modern API. Playwright excels at headless browsing, making it a valuable tool for web scraping dynamic websites.

1. What is Headless Browsing?

Headless browsing involves running a web browser without a graphical user interface (GUI). The browser operates in the background, executing JavaScript and rendering pages, but without displaying any visual output. This is particularly beneficial for web scraping, as it:

- **Increases Speed:** Eliminating the GUI rendering significantly speeds up page loading and scraping.
- **Reduces Resource Consumption:** Headless browsers consume fewer resources, allowing you to run more instances concurrently.
- **Simplifies Automation:** Headless browsing simplifies automation tasks, as you don't need to manage windows or visual interactions.

2. Playwright's Headless Mode

Playwright is designed with headless browsing in mind. It launches browsers in headless mode by default, making it easy to get started with scrapingdynamic content.

3. Installation and Setup

- **Install Playwright:**

Bash

```
npm install playwright
```

- **Install browser binaries:**

Bash

npx playwright install

This downloads the necessary browser binaries (Chromium, Firefox, and WebKit) for Playwright to use.

4. Basic Headless Scraping Example

JavaScript

```javascript
const { chromium } = require('playwright');

(async () => {
  // Launch a headless Chromium browser
  const browser = await chromium.launch();
  const page = await browser.newPage();

  // Navigate to the target URL
```

```javascript
  await page.goto('https://www.example.com');

  // Wait for the content to load (adjust selector as
needed)
  await page.waitForSelector('#content');

  // Extract data using CSS selectors
  const title = await page.$eval('h1', el =>
el.textContent);
  const price = await page.$eval('.price', el =>
el.textContent);

  console.log(`Title: ${title}`);
  console.log(`Price: ${price}`);

  await browser.close();
})();
```

This code demonstrates how to launch a headless Chromium browser, navigate to a URL, wait for specific content to load, and extract data using CSS selectors.

5. Key Features and Advantages

- **Auto-Waiting:** Playwright automatically waits for elements to be actionable before interacting with them, reducing the need for explicit waits.
- **Network Interception:** Intercept network requests to analyze or modify them, useful for understanding API calls or manipulating data.
- **Page Context:** Isolate different scraping tasks using separate page contexts, preventing interference and improving performance.
- **Debugging Tools:** Playwright provides debugging tools, including a visual inspector and a trace viewer, to help you understand and troubleshoot your scraping code.

6. Choosing Between Selenium and Playwright

- **Ease of Use:** Playwright's API is often considered more modern and intuitive than Selenium's.
- **Performance:** Playwright generally offers better performance and efficiency, especially in headless mode.

- **Browser Support:** Playwright supports a wider range of browsers (Chromium, Firefox, WebKit) out of the box.
- **Language Support:** Selenium has broader language support, while Playwright primarily focuses on JavaScript and Python.

By utilizing Playwright's headless browsing capabilities, you can efficiently scrape dynamic websites, access JavaScript-rendered content, and automate web interactions with ease. In the next section, we'll delve into techniques for handling AJAX requests and infinite scrolling, further expanding your web scraping arsenal.

Handling AJAX Requests and Infinite Scrolling

Many modern websites employ AJAX (Asynchronous JavaScript and XML) to load content dynamically and provide a smoother user experience. This technique allows web pages to update specific sections without requiring a full page reload. A common use case for AJAX is infinite scrolling, where new content loads as the user scrolls down the page. This section explores how to handle AJAX requests and infinite scrolling when scraping dynamic websites.

1. Understanding AJAX

AJAX enables web pages to send requests to the server in the background and update parts of the page with the received data. This is typically done using JavaScript and the XMLHttpRequest or fetch API.

Challenges for Scraping:

- **Hidden Content:** Content loaded via AJAX is often not present in the initial HTML source.
- **Network Requests:** Traditional scraping tools like requests only fetch the initial HTML and don't capture AJAX requests.

2. Scraping AJAX Content with Browser Automation

Browser automation tools like Selenium and Playwright are essential for scraping AJAX-driven content. They execute JavaScript, allowing you to:

- **Wait for AJAX Requests:** Wait for AJAX requests to complete and the content to be loaded before extracting data.
- **Simulate User Interactions:** If AJAX requests are triggered by user actions (e.g., clicking a button, scrolling), you can simulate those actions using Selenium or Playwright.
- **Intercept Network Requests:** Analyze and intercept network requests to understand how data is fetched and potentially access it directly.

3. Example: Scraping with Selenium

Python

```python
from selenium import webdriver

from selenium.webdriver.common.by import By

from selenium.webdriver.support.ui import WebDriverWait

from selenium.webdriver.support import expected_conditions as EC


# ... (Selenium setup) ...


# Navigate to the page with AJAX content

driver.get("https://www.example.com/ajax-content")


# Wait for the AJAX content to load (adjust selector as needed)

WebDriverWait(driver, 10).until(

EC.presence_of_element_located((By.CSS_SELECTOR, "#ajax-content"))
```

```
)
```

```python
# Extract the AJAX-loaded content
ajax_content                                    =
driver.find_element(By.CSS_SELECTOR,
"#ajax-content").text
```

```python
# ... (process the extracted data) ...
```

4. Handling Infinite Scrolling

Infinite scrolling presents a unique challenge, as new content continuously loads as you scroll. Here's a strategy for scraping infinite scrolling pages:

- **Scroll Down:** Use JavaScript within the browser automation tool to scroll down the page incrementally.
- **Wait for Content:** Wait for new content to load after each scroll.
- **Extract Data:** Extract the data from the newly loaded elements.
- **Repeat:** Repeat the process until no new content loads or you reach a desired limit.

Example (Playwright):

JavaScript

```javascript
const { chromium } = require('playwright');

(async () => {
  // ... (Playwright setup) ...

  await page.goto('https://www.example.com/infinite-scroll');

  let previousHeight;
  while (true) {

    previousHeight = await page.evaluate('document.body.scrollHeight');

    await page.evaluate('window.scrollTo(0, document.body.scrollHeight)');

    await page.waitForFunction(`document.body.scrollHeight > ${previousHeight}`);
```

```
// Extract data from newly loaded elements

// ...


      // Check if there's no more content or if you've
reached a limit

      // ...

   }


   await browser.close();

})();
```

5. Considerations

- **Website Structure:** Understand how the website implements infinite scrolling and identify the elements that signal new content loading.
- **Rate Limiting:** Be mindful of rate limits and avoid overloading the server with excessive scroll actions.
- **Efficiency:** Optimize your scrolling and waiting logic to avoid unnecessary delays and improve scraping speed.

By mastering these techniques, you can effectively scrape websites that use AJAX and infinite scrolling, expanding your ability to extract data from a wider range of dynamic web pages. In the next chapter, we'll explore how to interact with APIs, which provide a more structured and efficient way to access data from many websites.

Chapter 8: Interacting with APIs

Understanding Web APIs and RESTful Principles

Many websites offer Application Programming Interfaces (APIs) as a structured and efficient way to access their data.[1] APIs provide a programmatic interface for interacting with a web service, allowing you to request and receive data in a standardized format.[2] This chapter focuses on understanding web APIs, particularly those that adhere to RESTful principles, which have become the dominant standard for web API design.[3]

Understanding Web APIs and RESTful Principles

1. What is a Web API?

A web API is a set of rules and specifications that allow one application to access the features or data of another application.[4] It acts as an intermediary between two software systems, enabling them to communicate and exchange information.[5]

- **Client-Server Architecture:** APIs typically follow a client-server model, where the client (your web scraper) sends requests to the server (the application providing the API).[6]

- **Standardized Communication:** APIs define a standardized way for clients and servers to interact, often using HTTP (HyperText Transfer Protocol) for communication.[7]
- **Data Formats:** APIs commonly use data formats like JSON (JavaScript Object Notation) or XML (Extensible Markup Language) for exchanging information.[8]

2. RESTful APIs

REST (Representational State Transfer) is an architectural style for designing networked applications.[9] RESTful[10] APIs adhere to REST principles, providing a consistent and predictable way to interact with web services.[11]

Key Principles of REST:

- **Client-Server:** Clear separation between the client and the server.[12]
- **Stateless:** Each request from the client to the server must contain all the information necessary to understand the request.[13][14] The server does not store any client context between requests.[15]
- **Cacheable:** Responses from the server should explicitly state whether they can be cached or not, allowing clients to reuse responses and improve performance.[16]

- **Uniform Interface:** Defines a consistent way for clients to interact with the server, using standard HTTP methods (GET, POST, PUT, DELETE) and focusing on resources.[17]
- **Layered System:** The client does not need to know the internal implementation of the server, allowing for flexibility and scalability.[18]

3. Resources and Endpoints

In RESTful APIs, resources are the key abstractions.[19] A resource can be any object, data, or service that can be accessed via the API.[20] Each resource is identified by a unique URI (Uniform Resource Identifier), which is also known as the endpoint.[21]

- **Example:** /users (a collection of users), /users/123 (a specific user with ID 123), /products/456/reviews (reviews for a product with ID 456).

4. HTTP Methods

RESTful APIs use standard HTTP methods to perform actions on resources:[22]

- **GET:** Retrieve a resource or a collection of resources.[23]
- **POST:** Create a new resource.
- **PUT:** Update an existing resource.[2425]

- **DELETE:** Delete a resource.[2627]

5. Benefits of Using APIs

- **Efficiency:** APIs often provide a more efficient way to access data compared to web scraping, as they return data in a structured format.[28]
- **Data Integrity:** APIs provide access to reliable and up-to-date data directly from the source.
- **Scalability:** Well-designed APIs can handle a large number of requests, making them suitable for high-volume data extraction.[29]
- **Reduced Complexity:** Interacting with APIs can be less complex than web scraping, as you don't need to parse HTML or handle dynamic content.

By understanding web APIs and RESTful principles, you gain a valuable tool for accessing data from websites in a structured and efficient manner. In the next section, we'll explore how to make API requests with Python and work with the JSON data format commonly used in APIs.

Making API Requests with Python

Python's requests library, which we've used extensively for web scraping, is also an excellent tool for interacting with web APIs. This section explores how to use requests to make API requests, handle responses, and work with JSON data, which is a common format for API communication.

1. Sending API Requests

Making API requests with requests is similar to fetching web pages. You use the appropriate HTTP method (GET, POST, PUT, DELETE) to interact with the API endpoint.

- **GET Request:**

Python

```
import requests


url = "https://api.example.com/products"

response = requests.get(url)


# Check status code
if response.status_code == 200:
    # Process the response data
    print(response.json())
else:
```

```python
print(f"Error: {response.status_code}")
```

- **POST Request:**

Python

```python
url = "https://api.example.com/products"
data = {
    "name": "New Product",
    "price": 29.99
}
response = requests.post(url, json=data)
```

The json parameter automatically encodes the data as JSON and sets the Content-Type header to application/json.

2. Handling Responses

The response object provides methods to access the API's response:

- status_code: The HTTP status code (e.g., 200 OK, 201 Created, 400 Bad Request, 404 Not Found).
- json(): Decodes the JSON response into a Python dictionary or list.
- text: Returns the response content as a string.
- headers: A dictionary-like object containing the response headers.

3. Working with JSON Data

JSON (JavaScript Object Notation) is a lightweight data format commonly used in APIs. It represents data as key-value pairs and arrays.

- **Accessing Data:**

Python

```python
data = response.json()

product_name = data['name']

product_price = data['price']
```

- **Iterating through Arrays:**

Python

```python
products = response.json()
for product in products:
    print(product['name'])
```

4. API Parameters

Many APIs accept parameters to filter, sort, or paginate data.

- **Query Parameters:**

Python

```python
url = "https://api.example.com/products"
params = {
    "category": "electronics",
```

```python
    "limit": 10
}

response = requests.get(url, params=params)
```

- **Path Parameters:**

Python

```python
product_id = 123
url = f"https://api.example.com/products/{product_id}"
response = requests.get(url)
```

5. Authentication

Some APIs require authentication to access their data. Common authentication methods include API keys, OAuth, and basic authentication.

- **API Key:**

Python

```
url = "https://api.example.com/products"
headers = {
    "Authorization": "Bearer YOUR_API_KEY"
}
response = requests.get(url, headers=headers)
```

6. Error Handling

Implement error handling to gracefully handle potential API errors:

Python

```
try:
    response = requests.get(url)
    response.raise_for_status()  # Raise an exception for bad status codes
    data = response.json()
```

```
# ... process data ...

except requests.exceptions.RequestException as e:

    print(f"API request error: {e}")

except ValueError as e:

    print(f"JSON decoding error: {e}")
```

By mastering these techniques, you can effectively interact with APIs, retrieve data in a structured format, and integrate API data into your web scraping projects. In the next chapter, we'll explore how to overcome common challenges encountered when scraping websites, such as handling rate limits and CAPTCHAs.

Working with JSON and XML Data from APIs

APIs often use JSON (JavaScript Object Notation) or XML (Extensible Markup Language) to structure the data they return. This section explores how to work with these formats in Python when interacting with APIs.

1. JSON Data

JSON is a lightweight and human-readable data format that has become the most popular choice for APIs. It uses a simple syntax based on key-value pairs and arrays.

- **Parsing JSON with the** json **library:**

Python

```python
import requests
import json

response = requests.get("https://api.example.com/products")
data = response.json()

# Accessing data
print(data['name'])
print(data['price'])

# Iterating through an array
for item in data['items']:
    print(item['title'])
```

- **Key methods in the** json **library:**
  - json.loads(json_string): Parses a JSON string into a Python object (dictionary or list).
  - json.dumps(python_object): Converts a Python object into a JSON string.

2. XML Data

XML is another structured data format that uses tags to define elements and attributes to provide additional information. While less common in modern APIs, it's still used in some cases.

- **Parsing XML with** xml.etree.ElementTree**:**

Python

```
import requests

import xml.etree.ElementTree as ET


response = requests.get("https://api.example.com/products")
```

```
root = ET.fromstring(response.content)

# Accessing elements and attributes
name = root.find('name').text

price = root.find('price').text

currency = root.find('price').get('currency')
```

- **Key methods in** xml.etree.ElementTree**:**
  - ET.fromstring(xml_string): Parses an XML string into an ElementTree object.
  - root.find('element_name'): Finds the first child element with the given name.
  - root.findall('element_name'): Finds all child elements with the given name.
  - element.get('attribute_name'): Gets the value of an attribute.

3. Choosing Between JSON and XML

- **JSON:** Generally preferred for its simplicity, readability, and efficiency. It's well-supported in most programming languages and has become the standard for web APIs.

- **XML:** More verbose than JSON and can be less efficient to parse. It might be used in legacy systems or when specific features of XML (like namespaces or schemas) are required.

4. Handling Different Data Formats in Your Code

When working with APIs, you might encounter different data formats. You can check the Content-Type header in the response to determine the format and use the appropriate parsing library.

Python

```
if response.headers['Content-Type'] == 'application/json':

    data = response.json()

    # ... process JSON data ...

elif        response.headers['Content-Type']        ==
'application/xml':

    root = ET.fromstring(response.content)

    # ... process XML data ...
```

By understanding how to work with JSON and XML data, you can effectively extract information from APIs that use these formats and integrate that data into your applications or web scraping projects. In the next chapter, we'll explore techniques for overcoming common challenges encountered when scraping websites, such as handling rate limits and CAPTCHAs.

Authentication and API Keys

Many APIs require authentication to control access to their data and ensure that only authorized users can make requests. This section explores common authentication methods used in APIs, with a focus on API keys, one of the simplest and most widely used approaches.

1. Why APIs Need Authentication

- **Security:** Authentication protects API resources from unauthorized access and potential misuse.
- **Usage Control:** It allows API providers to track usage, enforce rate limits, and prevent abuse.
- **User Identification:** Authentication helps identify the user making the request, enabling personalized responses or access control to specific data.

2. API Keys

An API key is a unique identifier that is assigned to you (or your application) when you register with an API provider. It acts like a password, allowing the API to recognize and authenticate your requests.

- **How API Keys Work:**
  - You include the API key in your requests, typically in the headers or as a query parameter.
  - The API server verifies the key to ensure it's valid and associated with an authorized user.
- **Example with** requests:

Python

```
import requests

url = "https://api.example.com/data"

headers = {

    "Authorization": "Bearer YOUR_API_KEY"   # Include API key in header

}

response = requests.get(url, headers=headers)
```

3. Other Authentication Methods

- **Basic Authentication:** Involves sending username and password credentials with each request, usually encoded using Base64.
- **OAuth (Open Authorization):** A more secure and flexible method that allows users to grant third-party applications access to their resources without sharing their credentials.
- **JWT (JSON Web Tokens):** A compact and self-contained way to securely transmit information between parties as a JSON object.

4. API Key Best Practices

- **Secure Storage:** Store your API keys securely, avoid hardcoding them directly in your code, and consider using environment variables or configuration files.
- **Rate Limits:** Be aware of the API's rate limits and implement strategies to avoid exceeding them, such as introducing delays or using caching.
- **Key Rotation:** Periodically rotate your API keys to minimize the impact of a potential key compromise.

- **Least Privilege:** Use API keys with the least privilege necessary for your application.

5. Finding API Key Information

API providers typically document their authentication methods and how to obtain API keys in their developer documentation or API console.

6. Example: Using an API Key with a Weather API

Python

```
import requests


def get_weather(city, api_key):

    url = f"https://api.weatherapi.com/v1/current.json?key={api_key}&q={city}"

    response = requests.get(url)

    # ... (process weather data) ...
```

This example demonstrates how to use an API key to access a weather API and retrieve weather data for a given city.

By understanding authentication methods and how to use API keys, you can securely access a wide range of APIs and integrate their data into your applications or web scraping projects. In the next chapter, we'll explore how to overcome common challenges encountered when scraping websites, such as handling rate limits and CAPTCHAs.

Chapter 9: Overcoming Scraping Challenges

Handling Rate Limits and IP Blocking

Web scraping, while powerful, often presents challenges that require careful consideration and strategic solutions. This chapter addresses two common hurdles: handling rate limits and avoiding IP blocking. Mastering these techniques is essential for building robust and ethical scrapers that can reliably extract data without disrupting the target websites.

Handling Rate Limits and IP Blocking

1. Rate Limits

Many websites implement rate limits to control the number of requests they receive from a particular client within a specific timeframe. These limits prevent abuse, protect server resources, and ensure fair access for all users.

- **Identifying Rate Limits:** Websites might publish their rate limits in their API documentation or terms of service. However, sometimes you might need to deduce them through observation and experimentation.

- **Respecting Rate Limits:** Exceeding rate limits can lead to temporary or permanent blocking of your IP address. It's crucial to respect these limits to maintain access and ensure ethical scraping.

Techniques for Handling Rate Limits:

- **Introduce Delays:** Add delays between requests using time.sleep() in Python. Adjust the delay based on the observed rate limit.

Python

```python
import time

time.sleep(2)  # Wait for 2 seconds between requests
```

- **Exponential Backoff:** Gradually increase the delay between requests if you encounter rate limit errors. This allows the server to recover and prevents aggressive retrying.
- **Leaky Bucket Algorithm:** Implement a mechanism to control the rate of requests, similar to how a leaky bucket regulates the flow of water.

- **Token Bucket Algorithm:** Another rate-limiting algorithm that allows bursts of requests within a defined limit.
- **Respect** Retry-After **Headers:** If the server sends a Retry-After header in the response, adhere to the specified delay before making further requests.

2. IP Blocking

Websites might block your IP address if they detect suspicious activity, such as:

- **High Request Frequency:** Making too many requests in a short period.
- **User-Agent Spoofing:** Using a fake or misleading User-Agent header.
- **Scraping Prohibited Content:** Accessing pages or data that are explicitly prohibited from scraping (e.g., by robots.txt).

Techniques for Avoiding IP Blocking:

- **Rotate IP Addresses:** Use a proxy server or a pool of proxies to distribute your requests across different IP addresses.
- **Set Realistic User-Agents:** Use a User-Agent header that mimics a real web browser to avoid detection.

- **Adhere to robots.txt:** Respect the website's robots.txt rules and avoid scraping disallowed content.
- **Spread Requests Over Time:** Avoid concentrated bursts of requests. Distribute your scraping tasks over longer periods.
- **Monitor for Blocking:** Implement mechanisms to detect IP blocking (e.g., checking for specific status codes or error messages) and adjust your strategy accordingly.

3. Ethical Considerations

- **Respect Website Terms:** Always review and adhere to the website's terms of service and scraping policy.
- **Minimize Impact:** Avoid overloading the server with excessive requests. Scrape responsibly and consider the website's resources.
- **Data Privacy:** Be mindful of scraping personal or sensitive data. Ensure compliance with privacy regulations.

4. Example: Rotating Proxies with requests

Python

```
import requests
```

```python
proxies = {
    'http': 'http://user:password@proxy1.example.com:port',
    'https': 'https://user:password@proxy2.example.com:port'
}

response = requests.get("https://www.example.com", proxies=proxies)
```

This example demonstrates how to use proxy servers with the requests library to rotate IP addresses and reduce the risk of blocking.

By understanding and implementing these techniques, you can build resilient web scrapers that can handle rate limits, avoid IP blocking, and ethically extract data without disrupting the target websites. In the next section, we'll explore how to use proxies for anonymity and access websites that might be geographically restricted.

Using Proxies for Anonymity and Access

Proxies act as intermediaries between your computer and the internet. When you use a proxy, your web requests are routed through the proxy server before reaching the target website. This has several benefits for web scraping, including anonymity and bypassing geo-restrictions.

1. How Proxies Work

- **Request Routing:** When you send a web request through a proxy, the request goes to the proxy server first.
- **IP Masking:** The proxy server then forwards the request to the target website, but the website sees the proxy server's IP address instead of your actual IP address.
- **Response Forwarding:** The website's response is sent back to the proxy server, which then forwards it to your computer.

2. Types of Proxies

- **HTTP Proxies:** Work at the application layer and are suitable for basic web scraping tasks.
- **HTTPS Proxies:** Support encrypted HTTPS connections, providing additional security.

- **SOCKS5 Proxies:** Operate at a lower level (session layer) and can handle various types of traffic, including HTTP, HTTPS, and FTP.

3. Benefits for Web Scraping

- **Anonymity:** Proxies mask your IP address, making it harder for websites to track your scraping activity.
- **Geo-Restriction Bypassing:** Use proxies located in different countries to access websites or content that might be blocked in your region.
- **IP Rotation:** Utilize a pool of proxies to rotate your IP address with each request, reducing the risk of rate limiting or IP blocking.

4. Choosing the Right Proxy

- **Free vs. Paid:** Free proxies are often unreliable and slow. Paid proxies generally offer better performance, security, and anonymity.
- **Location:** Choose proxies located in the region you need to access or in a location that is less likely to be blocked.
- **Type:** Select the proxy type (HTTP, HTTPS, SOCKS5) based on your scraping needs and the website's requirements.
- **Rotation:** Consider using a proxy rotation service to automatically switch between different proxies.

5. Using Proxies with requests

Python

```
import requests


# Configure the proxy
proxies = {
    'http': 'http://user:password@proxy.example.com:port',
                                                    'https':
'https://user:password@proxy.example.com:port'
}


# Send a request through the proxy
response = requests.get("https://www.example.com",
proxies=proxies)
```

6. Ethical Considerations

- **Respect Proxy Usage Policies:** Adhere to the terms of service of the proxy provider.

- **Avoid Malicious Activities:** Don't use proxies for illegal or unethical purposes.
- **Privacy Concerns:** Be aware that some proxies might log your activity. Choose reputable providers if privacy is a concern.

By incorporating proxies into your web scraping strategy, you can enhance your anonymity, bypass geographic restrictions, and build more resilient scrapers that can access data from a wider range of sources. In the next section, we'll explore techniques for solving CAPTCHAs, another common challenge encountered during web scraping.

CAPTCHA Solving Techniques

CAPTCHAs (Completely Automated Public Turing test to tell Computers and Humans Apart) are designed to prevent automated bots from accessing websites or submitting forms. They present challenges that require human-like perception and problem-solving abilities, such as identifying distorted text, recognizing images, or solving simple puzzles. This section explores techniques for handling CAPTCHAs in your web scraping projects.

1. Types of CAPTCHAs

- **Text-based CAPTCHAs:** Present distorted or obscured text that users need to decipher.

- **Image-based CAPTCHAs:** Require users to identify objects, scenes, or patterns in images.
- **Audio CAPTCHAs:** Play distorted audio recordings of words or numbers that users need to transcribe.
- **reCAPTCHA:** A sophisticated CAPTCHA system developed by Google that uses various challenges, including image recognition and behavioral analysis.

2. CAPTCHA Solving Techniques

- **Optical Character Recognition (OCR):** For text-based CAPTCHAs, OCR libraries like Tesseract can be used to recognize the distorted text. However, OCR accuracy can vary depending on the complexity of the distortion.
- **Image Recognition APIs:** Services like Google Cloud Vision API or Amazon Rekognition can be used to analyze image-based CAPTCHAs and identify objects or patterns.
- **Third-Party CAPTCHA Solving Services:** Several services specialize in solving CAPTCHAs using human workers or advanced algorithms. These services can provide solutions via APIs, but they often come with costs and ethical considerations.
- **Audio Transcription APIs:** For audio CAPTCHAs, speech-to-text APIs like Google

Cloud Speech-to-Text can be used to transcribe the audio.

3. Implementing CAPTCHA Solving

- **Integration with Scraping Tools:** Integrate CAPTCHA solving techniques into your scraping workflow using browser automation tools like Selenium or Playwright.
- **Handling CAPTCHA Detection:** Implement logic to detect when a CAPTCHA is presented and trigger the appropriate solving mechanism.
- **Fallback Mechanisms:** Provide fallback mechanisms, such as manual solving or using a CAPTCHA solving service, if automated solutions fail.

4. Example: Using a CAPTCHA Solving Service

Python

```
from selenium import webdriver

# ... (Selenium setup) ...


# ... (navigate to page with CAPTCHA) ...


# Get the CAPTCHA image URL
```

```python
captcha_img        =        driver.find_element(By.ID,
"captcha_image")

captcha_url = captcha_img.get_attribute("src")


# Send the CAPTCHA image to a solving service API

response                                              =
requests.post("https://captcha-solver.com/api",
data={"image": captcha_url})

captcha_solution = response.json()["solution"]


# Enter the solution into the CAPTCHA field

captcha_field        =        driver.find_element(By.ID,
"captcha_input")

captcha_field.send_keys(captcha_solution)


# ... (submit the form) ...
```

5. Ethical and Legal Considerations

- **Website Terms of Service:** Review the website's terms of service to ensure that automated CAPTCHA solving is not prohibited.
- **CAPTCHA Purpose:** Understand the purpose of the CAPTCHA and consider whether bypassing it is ethical or necessary for your use case.
- **Service Abuse:** Avoid abusing CAPTCHA solving services, as this can lead to account suspension or legal issues.

By understanding CAPTCHA solving techniques and implementing them responsibly, you can overcome this common web scraping challenge and access websites that employ CAPTCHAs for security. However, always prioritize ethical considerations and respect website terms of service when implementing CAPTCHA bypass mechanisms.

Scraping Data from JavaScript-Heavy Websites

Modern websites increasingly rely on JavaScript to create dynamic and interactive user experiences. This poses a challenge for traditional web scraping techniques that primarily focus on extracting data from static HTML. This section explores strategies for effectively scraping data from JavaScript-heavy websites.

1. Challenges of JavaScript-Heavy Websites

- **Dynamic Content Rendering:** JavaScript frameworks and libraries like React, Angular, and Vue.js render content on the client-side, meaning the data you need might not be present in the initial HTML source code.
- **API Calls and AJAX:** Websites often use JavaScript to make API calls and fetch data asynchronously, making it difficult to capture the complete data flow with traditional scraping tools.
- **Complex Interactions:** JavaScript-heavy websites might involve complex user interactions, animations, and dynamic updates that can be challenging to automate.

2. Essential Techniques

- **Browser Automation:** Tools like Selenium and Playwright are crucial for scraping JavaScript-heavy websites. They allow you to control a browser programmatically, execute JavaScript, and render dynamic content.
- **Headless Browsing:** Run the browser in headless mode to increase speed and reduce resource consumption.
- **Waiting Strategies:** Implement explicit waits to ensure that elements are rendered and interactable before attempting to extract data.

- **Network Interception:** Use browser automation tools to intercept network requests and analyze API calls to understand how data is fetched and potentially access it directly.
- **Reverse Engineering:** In some cases, you might need to inspect and understand the website's JavaScript code to determine how data is generated and how to extract it effectively.

3. Example: Scraping a Single-Page Application (SPA)

Python

```python
from selenium import webdriver

from selenium.webdriver.common.by import By

from selenium.webdriver.support.ui import WebDriverWait

from selenium.webdriver.support import expected_conditions as EC


# ... (Selenium setup) ...


# Navigate to the SPA
```

```python
driver.get("https://www.example.com/spa")


# Wait for the content to load (adjust selector as needed)

WebDriverWait(driver, 10).until(


EC.presence_of_element_located((By.CSS_SELECTOR
, "#app-container"))

)


# Extract data after JavaScript rendering

data    =    driver.find_element(By.CSS_SELECTOR,
"#data-element").text


# ... (process the extracted data) ...
```

4. Best Practices

- **Choose the Right Tool:** Select the appropriate browser automation tool (Selenium, Playwright) based on your needs and the website's complexity.

- **Optimize for Performance:** Use headless browsing, efficient locators, and optimized waiting strategies to improve scraping speed.
- **Respect Website Terms:** Adhere to the website's terms of service and robots.txt to avoid being blocked.
- **Ethical Considerations:** Scrape responsibly and avoid overloading the server with excessive requests.

5. Advanced Techniques

- **JavaScript Evaluation:** Use driver.execute_script() in Selenium or page.evaluate() in Playwright to execute JavaScript code within the browser context and extract data or manipulate the page.
- **Debugging Tools:** Utilize browser developer tools and debugging features in your automation tools to understand the website's behavior and troubleshoot scraping issues.

By mastering these techniques and tools, you can effectively scrape data from JavaScript-heavy websites, access dynamically rendered content, and extract valuable information from modern web applications.

Part IV: Data Handling and Scalability

Chapter 10: Data Cleaning and Processing

Cleaning and Transforming Scraped Data

Web scraping often yields raw data that requires cleaning and transformation before it can be used for analysis or other purposes.[1] This chapter explores essential techniques for cleaning and transforming scraped data, ensuring its accuracy, consistency, and usability.

Cleaning and Transforming Scraped Data

Raw scraped data can contain inconsistencies, errors, and unwanted artifacts that need to be addressed before the data becomes truly valuable.[2] Cleaning and transforming this data is a crucial step in the web scraping process.

1. Common Data Issues

- **HTML Tags and Markup:** Scraped data might contain HTML tags, attributes, and other markup that need to be removed or handled.[3]
- **Inconsistent Formatting:** Data might be inconsistently formatted, such as dates in different formats, prices with varying currency symbols, or text with inconsistent capitalization.[4]

- **Missing Values:** Some data fields might be missing or incomplete.[5]
- **Duplicate Entries:** The scraping process might inadvertently collect duplicate entries.[6]
- **Irrelevant Information:** The scraped data might include irrelevant information that needs to be filtered out.[7]
- **Encoding Issues:** Text data might have encoding issues that need to be resolved to ensure proper character representation.[8]

2. Cleaning Techniques

- **Removing HTML Tags:** Use Beautiful Soup's get_text() method or regular expressions to remove HTML tags while preserving the text content.

Python

```
from bs4 import BeautifulSoup

html = "<p>This is <b>bold</b> text.</p>"

soup = BeautifulSoup(html, 'html.parser')

text = soup.get_text()  # Output: This is bold text.
```

- **Handling Missing Values:** Decide how to handle missing values. Options include:
  - Removing rows or columns with missing data.[9]
  - Filling missing values with a default value (e.g., "N/A").
  - Imputing missing values using statistical methods (e.g., mean, median).[10]
- **Removing Duplicate Entries:** Identify and remove duplicate entries based on unique identifiers or key fields.[11]
- **Standardizing Formats:** Convert data to consistent formats, such as:
  - Dates: 2024-12-31
  - Prices: 19.99
  - Text: Sentence case.
- **Filtering Data:** Use conditional statements or filtering functions to remove irrelevant information.
- **Regular Expressions:** Powerful tools for pattern matching and text manipulation.[12] Use them for tasks like:
  - Extracting specific parts of a string.[13]
  - Replacing patterns with desired values.
  - Validating data formats.

3. Data Transformation

Data transformation involves converting data from one format or structure to another to make it more suitable for analysis or storage.[14]

- **Data Type Conversion:** Convert data types as needed, such as strings to numbers, dates to timestamps, or lists to dictionaries.[15]
- **Data Normalization:** Scale numerical data to a common range to improve comparability.[16]
- **Data Aggregation:** Group and summarize data to gain insights (e.g., calculating averages, sums, or counts).
- **Feature Engineering:** Create new features or variables from existing data to improve analysis or machine learning model performance.[17]

4. Tools for Data Cleaning and Transformation

- **Python Libraries:**
    - **Pandas:** Provides powerful data manipulation capabilities, including data cleaning, transformation, and analysis.[18]
    - **NumPy:** Offers numerical computing tools for efficient array operations.[19]
    - **Regular Expressions:** Built-in re module for pattern matching and text manipulation.

5. Example: Cleaning and Transforming Product Data

Python

```
import pandas as pd

# Sample product data (with inconsistencies)
data = {
    'name': ['Product A', 'Product B ', ' product c'],
    'price': ['$20.50', '25', '€18.99'],
    'description':    ['<p>Description    with
<b>HTML</b>.</p>', 'Another description.', None]
}


df = pd.DataFrame(data)


# Clean and transform the data
df['name'] = df['name'].str.strip().str.title()  # Standardize
names
```

```
df['price']  =  df['price'].astype(str).str.replace(r'[^\d.]', '',
regex=True)  # Extract numeric price

df['price']  =  pd.to_numeric(df['price'])    #  Convert  to
numeric

df['description']                                              =
df['description'].astype(str).str.replace(r'<[^>]+>',        '',
regex=True)  # Remove HTML tags


print(df)
```

This example demonstrates how to use Pandas to clean
and transform product data, including standardizing
names, extracting numeric prices, and removing HTML
tags from descriptions.

By mastering data cleaning and transformation
techniques, you can ensure that your scraped data is
accurate, consistent, and ready for analysis,
visualization, or storage in databases.

Data Validation and Error Handling

Data validation and error handling are essential aspects
of data cleaning and processing. They ensure that your
scraped data is accurate, reliable, and consistent,

preventing errors and inconsistencies from propagating through your analysis or applications.

1. Data Validation

Data validation involves checking whether the scraped data conforms to predefined rules or constraints. This helps identify and correct invalid or inconsistent data.

- **Validation Techniques:**
    - **Data Type Validation:** Verify that data is of the correct type (e.g., integer, float, string, date).
    - **Range Checks:** Ensure that numerical data falls within an acceptable range.
    - **Format Validation:** Check that data adheres to specific formatting rules (e.g., email addresses, phone numbers, dates).
    - **Code Validation:** Validate codes or identifiers against known values or patterns.
    - **Cross-Field Validation:** Verify consistency between related data fields.
    - **Custom Validation:** Implement custom validation rules based on specific requirements.

2. Error Handling

Error handling involves gracefully managing errors or exceptions that might occur during data cleaning and processing. This prevents your code from crashing and allows you to handle invalid data appropriately.

- **Error Handling Techniques:**
    - try-except **Blocks:** Use try-except blocks to catch exceptions and handle them gracefully.
    - **Logging:** Log errors and warnings to track issues and aid in debugging.
    - **Data Replacement or Correction:** Attempt to replace or correct invalid data based on predefined rules or heuristics.
    - **Data Removal:** Remove invalid or inconsistent data if it cannot be corrected.
    - **User Notification:** If appropriate, notify users about data validation errors or provide feedback on how to correct them.

3. Example: Validating and Handling Product Data

Python

```python
import pandas as pd


# ... (sample product data) ...
```

```python
def validate_price(price):
    try:
        price = float(price)
        if price > 0:
            return price
        else:
            raise ValueError("Price must be positive.")
    except ValueError as e:
        print(f"Invalid price: {e}")
        return None


# Apply validation and error handling
df['price'] = df['price'].apply(validate_price)
df.dropna(subset=['price'], inplace=True)   # Remove rows with invalid prices


print(df)
```

This example demonstrates how to validate prices, ensuring they are positive numbers. It uses a try-except block to handle potential errors and removes rows with invalid prices.

4. Benefits of Data Validation and Error Handling

- **Data Quality:** Ensures that your data is accurate, consistent, and reliable.
- **Error Prevention:** Prevents errors from propagating through your analysis or applications.
- **Code Robustness:** Makes your code more robust and less prone to crashes.
- **Maintainability:** Improves code maintainability by providing clear error handling mechanisms.

By incorporating data validation and error handling into your data cleaning and processing workflow, you can significantly enhance the quality and reliability of your scraped data, leading to more accurate insights and better decision-making.

Working with Pandas for Data Manipulation

Pandas is a powerful Python library that provides high-performance, easy-to-use data structures and data analysis tools. It's particularly well-suited for working with structured data, making it an invaluable asset for manipulating and analyzing scraped data. This section explores how to leverage Pandas for efficient data manipulation in your web scraping projects.

1. DataFrames: The Foundation of Pandas

The core data structure in Pandas is the DataFrame. It's a two-dimensional table-like structure with rows and columns, similar to a spreadsheet or SQL table. DataFrames provide a flexible and intuitive way to organize, manipulate, and analyze data.

Creating DataFrames:

- **From a dictionary:**

Python

```python
import pandas as pd

data = {
    'name': ['Product A', 'Product B', 'Product C'],
    'price': [20.50, 25.00, 18.99],
    'rating': [4.5, 4.2, 4.8]
}
```

```python
df = pd.DataFrame(data)
```

- **From a list of lists:**

Python

```python
data = [
    ['Product A', 20.50, 4.5],
    ['Product B', 25.00, 4.2],
    ['Product C', 18.99, 4.8]
]
df = pd.DataFrame(data, columns=['name', 'price', 'rating'])
```

- **From a CSV file:**

Python

```
df = pd.read_csv('products.csv')
```

2. Essential Data Manipulation Operations

- **Accessing Data:**
  - **Selecting columns:** df['name'], df[['name', 'price']]
  - **Filtering rows:** df[df['price'] > 20]
  - **Indexing:** df.iloc[0], df.loc[df['name'] == 'Product A']
- **Data Cleaning:**
  - **Handling missing values:** df.fillna(0), df.dropna()
  - **Removing duplicates:** df.drop_duplicates()
- **Data Transformation:**
  - **Adding columns:** df['new_column'] = df['price'] * 0.8
  - **Applying functions:** df['price'].apply(lambda x: x * 1.1)
  - **Grouping and aggregation:** df.groupby('category')['price'].mean()
- **Data Export:**
  - **Saving to CSV:** df.to_csv('processed_products.csv')

- Saving to Excel: df.to_excel('products.xlsx')

3. Example: Analyzing Scraped Product Data

Python

```python
import pandas as pd


# ... (assume df contains scraped product data) ...


# Calculate the average price
average_price = df['price'].mean()
print(f"Average Price: {average_price}")


# Find the most expensive product
most_expensive = df.loc[df['price'].idxmax()]
print(f"Most Expensive Product: {most_expensive['name']}")


# Group products by category and calculate the average price for each category
```

```
category_prices = df.groupby('category')['price'].mean()

print(category_prices)
```

This example demonstrates how to use Pandas to calculate the average price, find the most expensive product, and group products by category to analyze price trends.

4. Benefits of Using Pandas

- **Efficiency:** Pandas is built for performance, handling large datasets efficiently.
- **Flexibility:** Provides a wide range of data manipulation tools and functions.
- **Ease of Use:** Offers an intuitive API and integrates well with other Python libraries.
- **Data Analysis:** Provides functionalities for data analysis, exploration, and visualization.

By incorporating Pandas into your web scraping workflow, you can efficiently clean, transform, and analyze scraped data, extracting valuable insights and making data-driven decisions.

Chapter 11: Data Storage and Management

Storing Data in CSV Files

Once you've scraped and processed your data, you need a reliable way to store and manage it. This chapter focuses on one of the simplest and most versatile data storage formats: CSV files. We'll explore how to store your scraped data in CSV files, the benefits of this approach, and best practices for managing your data effectively.

Storing Data in CSV Files

CSV (Comma-Separated Values) files are plain text files that store tabular data (numbers and text) in a structured format. Each line in a CSV file represents a row of data, and values within a row are separated by commas (or another delimiter). This simplicity and human-readable nature make CSV files a popular choice for storing and exchanging data.

1. Structure of a CSV File

- **Header Row (Optional):** The first row often contains column headers, providing names for each data field.

- **Data Rows:** Subsequent rows contain the actual data values, with each value separated by a comma.
- **Delimiter:** While commas are the most common delimiter, other characters like tabs, semicolons, or pipes can also be used.
- **Example:**

Code snippet

name,price,category

Product A,20.50,Electronics

Product B,15.99,Books

Product C,125.00,Clothing

2. Writing Data to CSV with Python

Python's csv module provides functionalities for working with CSV files.

- **Using the** csv.writer**:**

Python

```python
import csv

data = [
    ['name', 'price', 'category'],
    ['Product A', 20.50, 'Electronics'],
    ['Product B', 15.99, 'Books'],
    ['Product C', 125.00, 'Clothing']
]

with open('products.csv', 'w', newline='') as csvfile:
    writer = csv.writer(csvfile)
    writer.writerows(data)  # Write all rows at once
```

- **Writing data row by row:**

Python

```python
with open('products.csv', 'w', newline='') as csvfile:
```

```python
    writer = csv.writer(csvfile)

    writer.writerow(['name', 'price', 'category'])  # Write
header

    for product in products:

        writer.writerow([product['name'], product['price'],
product['category']])
```

3. Reading Data from CSV with Python

- **Using the** csv.reader**:**

Python

```python
with open('products.csv', 'r') as csvfile:

    reader = csv.reader(csvfile)

    for row in reader:

        print(row)
```

4. Working with Pandas

Pandas provides a more convenient way to read and write CSV files, especially when dealing with large datasets or complex data manipulation.

- **Writing to CSV:**

Python

```python
import pandas as pd


df = pd.DataFrame(data)   # Assuming data is a list of lists or a dictionary

df.to_csv('products.csv', index=False)   # index=False prevents writing row indices
```

- **Reading from CSV:**

Python

```python
df = pd.read_csv('products.csv')
```

5. Benefits of CSV Files

- **Simplicity:** Easy to understand and work with, even without specialized tools.
- **Portability:** Can be opened and processed by various applications, including spreadsheets and text editors.
- **Versatility:** Suitable for storing a wide range of tabular data.
- **Version Control:** Plain text format makes it easy to track changes with version control systems.

6. Best Practices

- **Choose an Appropriate Delimiter:** If your data contains commas, use a different delimiter (e.g., tab, semicolon) to avoid ambiguity.
- **Handle Special Characters:** Properly escape or quote values that contain commas, newlines, or quotes within the data.
- **Use UTF-8 Encoding:** Ensure consistent character encoding by using UTF-8.
- **Data Validation:** Validate your data before storing it to maintain data integrity.

By understanding how to work with CSV files in Python, you gain a reliable and versatile method for storing and managing your scraped data. In the next chapter, we'll explore more advanced data storage options, including databases.

Introduction to Databases (SQL and NoSQL)

While CSV files are suitable for basic data storage, databases offer more advanced features for managing, querying, and scaling your scraped data. This section provides an introduction to databases, exploring the two main categories: SQL and NoSQL databases.

1. What is a Database?

A database is an organized collection of data that is stored and accessed electronically. Databases are designed for efficient data management, providing features like:

- **Structured Storage:** Data is organized into tables with rows and columns, allowing for structured queries and analysis.
- **Data Integrity:** Databases enforce constraints and rules to maintain data consistency and accuracy.
- **Efficient Retrieval:** Databases use indexing and optimization techniques to retrieve data quickly.

- **Concurrency Control:** Databases handle concurrent access from multiple users or applications, ensuring data consistency.
- **Scalability:** Databases can scale to handle large volumes of data and high traffic loads.

2. SQL Databases

SQL (Structured Query Language) databases are relational databases that store data in tables with predefined schemas. They use SQL as the language for defining, querying, and manipulating data.

- **Key Characteristics:**
  - **Structured Data:** Data is organized into tables with rows and columns.
  - **Schema:** Tables have a predefined schema that defines the data types and constraints for each column.
  - **Relationships:** Tables can be related to each other through foreign keys, enabling efficient querying and data integrity.
  - **ACID Properties:** SQL databases guarantee Atomicity, Consistency, Isolation, and Durability, ensuring reliable transactions.
- **Popular SQL Databases:**
  - MySQL
  - PostgreSQL

- ○ SQLite
- ○ Microsoft SQL Server
- ○ Oracle Database

3. NoSQL Databases

NoSQL (Not Only SQL) databases provide a flexible and scalable alternative to traditional SQL databases. They are designed to handle unstructured or semi-structured data and scale horizontally across multiple servers.

- **Key Characteristics:**
  - ○ **Flexible Schema:** NoSQL databases often have flexible or dynamic schemas, allowing you to store data with varying structures.
  - ○ **Horizontal Scalability:** NoSQL databases can easily scale horizontally by distributing data across multiple servers.
  - ○ **Variety of Data Models:** NoSQL databases support various data models, including:
    - ■ **Document databases:** Store data in documents, often in JSON or XML format (e.g., MongoDB).
    - ■ **Key-value stores:** Store data as key-value pairs (e.g., Redis, Memcached).

- **Graph databases:** Represent data as nodes and relationships (e.g., Neo4j).
- **Wide-column stores:** Store data in columns grouped into column families (e.g., Cassandra).
- **Popular NoSQL Databases:**
  - MongoDB
  - Cassandra
  - Redis
  - Amazon DynamoDB

4. Choosing the Right Database

- **SQL Databases:** Suitable for applications that require:
  - Structured data with relationships.
  - ACID properties and strong data consistency.
  - Complex queries and joins.
- **NoSQL Databases:** Suitable for applications that require:
  - Flexible schema and handling of unstructured data.
  - Horizontal scalability and high availability.
  - High write throughput and low latency.

5. Connecting to Databases with Python

Python provides libraries for connecting to and interacting with various databases:

- **SQL Databases:**
    - sqlite3 (for SQLite)
    - mysql.connector (for MySQL)
    - psycopg2 (for PostgreSQL)
- **NoSQL Databases:**
    - pymongo (for MongoDB)
    - cassandra-driver (for Cassandra)
    - redis (for Redis)

By understanding the fundamentals of SQL and NoSQL databases, you can make informed decisions about the best data storage solution for your web scraping projects. In the next section, we'll explore how to choose the right database based on your specific needs.

Choosing the Right Database for Your Needs

Selecting the appropriate database for your web scraping project is crucial for efficient data management, scalability, and performance. This section provides guidance on choosing between SQL and NoSQL databases based on your specific requirements.

1. Factors to Consider

- **Data Structure:**

- ○ **Structured Data:** If your data is highly structured with clear relationships between entities (e.g., products, customers, orders), an SQL database is often a good fit.
- ○ **Unstructured or Semi-structured Data:** For data with varying structures or formats (e.g., social media posts, sensor data, log files), a NoSQL database might be more suitable.
- **Scalability:**
  - ○ **Vertical Scaling:** SQL databases typically scale vertically by increasing the resources (CPU, memory, storage) of a single server.
  - ○ **Horizontal Scaling:** NoSQL databases often excel at horizontal scaling, distributing data across multiple servers to handle increased load.
- **Data Consistency:**
  - ○ **ACID Properties:** SQL databases guarantee ACID properties (Atomicity, Consistency, Isolation, Durability), ensuring strong data consistency and reliable transactions.
  - ○ **Eventual Consistency:** Some NoSQL databases prioritize availability and partition tolerance over strong

consistency, leading to eventual consistency[1] where data might not be immediately consistent across all replicas.

- **Query Patterns:**
  - **Complex Queries and Joins:** SQL databases are well-suited for complex queries that involve joining data from multiple tables.
  - **Simple Lookups and Key-Based Access:** NoSQL databases like key-value stores excel at fast lookups based on keys.
- **Data Volume and Velocity:**
  - **High Volume and Velocity:** NoSQL databases are often preferred for handling high-volume, high-velocity data, such as real-time data streams or large datasets.
- **Development and Maintenance:**
  - **Schema Management:** SQL databases require defining a schema upfront, which can be more rigid but provides data integrity.
  - **Flexibility:** NoSQL databases offer more flexibility with schema design, but might require more careful data modeling.

2. Decision Matrix

Feature	SQL Databases	NoSQL Databases
Data Structure	Structured	Unstructured/Semi-structured
Scalability	Vertical	Horizontal
Consistency	ACID properties	Eventual consistency (in some cases)
Query Patterns	Complex queries, joins	Simple lookups, key-based access
Data Volume/Velocity	Moderate	High
Schema	Fixed	Flexible

3. Examples

- **E-commerce Product Catalog:** An SQL database would be suitable for storing product information, categories, customer data, and orders due to the structured nature of the data and relationships between entities.
- **Social Media Analytics:** A NoSQL database (e.g., a document database) would be a good choice for storing social media posts, user

profiles, and interactions due to the unstructured nature of the data and the need for flexible schema.

- **Real-time Sensor Data:** A NoSQL database (e.g., a time-series database) would be appropriate for storing and analyzing high-velocity sensor data due to its scalability and ability to handle time-stamped data.

4. Hybrid Approach

In some cases, a hybrid approach using both SQL and NoSQL databases might be beneficial. For example, you could use an SQL database for structured transactional data and a NoSQL database for unstructured data like user reviews or social media feeds.

By carefully considering these factors and evaluating your specific requirements, you can choose the database that best aligns with your web scraping project's needs, ensuring efficient data storage, management, and scalability.

Chapter 12: Building Scalable Web Scrapers

Designing for Scalability and Maintainability

As your web scraping needs grow, you'll need to design scrapers that can handle increasing amounts of data, changing website structures, and potential errors. This chapter focuses on designing scalable and maintainable web scrapers that can adapt to evolving requirements and remain robust over time.

Designing for Scalability and Maintainability

Scalability refers to a scraper's ability to handle growing amounts of data and increasing complexity without significant performance degradation. Maintainability ensures that your scraper is easy to understand, modify, and update as needed.

1. Key Principles

- **Modularity:** Break down your scraper into smaller, independent modules or functions with clear responsibilities. This improves code organization, reusability, and testability.
- **Separation of Concerns:** Separate different aspects of your scraper, such as data extraction,

cleaning, processing, and storage, into distinct modules.

- **Configuration:** Use configuration files or environment variables to store settings like URLs, API keys, and scraping parameters. This allows you to easily modify settings without changing the code.
- **Abstraction:** Abstract away implementation details behind well-defined interfaces. This allows you to change the underlying implementation without affecting other parts of the scraper.
- **Error Handling:** Implement robust error handling to gracefully handle exceptions, network issues, and unexpected data formats.
- **Logging:** Use logging to track events, errors, and progress, providing valuable insights into the scraper's operation.

2. Scalability Strategies

- **Concurrency:** Utilize concurrency techniques (threading, asynchronous programming) to fetch and process multiple pages concurrently, significantly improving speed.
- **Distributed Scraping:** For large-scale scraping, consider distributing tasks across multiple machines or using cloud-based solutions like AWS Lambda or Google Cloud Functions.

- **Caching:** Implement caching mechanisms to store previously scraped data, reducing the need to repeatedly fetch the same information.
- **Database Storage:** Use databases (SQL or NoSQL) for efficient data storage, retrieval, and management, especially for large datasets.
- **Message Queues:** For complex workflows, use message queues (e.g., RabbitMQ, Celery) to decouple tasks and improve scalability.

3. Maintainability Best Practices

- **Code Style and Documentation:** Follow consistent code style guidelines and write clear documentation to make your code understandable and maintainable.
- **Version Control:** Use a version control system (e.g., Git) to track changes, collaborate with others, and revert to previous versions if needed.
- **Testing:** Write unit tests to verify the functionality of individual modules and ensure code correctness.
- **Refactoring:** Regularly refactor your code to improve its structure, readability, and efficiency.

4. Example: Modular Scraper Design

Python

scraper.py (main script)

```python
from modules import data_extraction, data_cleaning, data_storage


def main():
    config = load_config()   # Load settings from a configuration file
    urls = get_urls_from_config(config)

    for url in urls:
        raw_data = data_extraction.scrape_page(url)
        cleaned_data = data_cleaning.clean_data(raw_data)
        data_storage.store_data(cleaned_data, config)


if __name__ == "__main__":
    main()


# modules/data_extraction.py
import requests
from bs4 import BeautifulSoup
```

```
def scrape_page(url):

    # ... (code to fetch and extract data) ...

    return extracted_data



# ... (other modules for data cleaning and storage) ...
```

This example demonstrates a modular design where data extraction, cleaning, and storage are separated into different modules, improving code organization and maintainability.

5. Continuous Improvement

- **Monitoring:** Monitor your scraper's performance, identify bottlenecks, and optimize code as needed.
- **Adaptability:** Design your scraper to be adaptable to changes in website structure or data formats.
- **Code Reviews:** Conduct code reviews to identify potential issues and improve code quality.

By following these principles and strategies, you can build scalable and maintainable web scrapers that can adapt to evolving requirements, handle large datasets, and remain robust over time.

Using Message Queues (e.g., RabbitMQ, Celery)

Message queues provide a powerful mechanism for building scalable and robust web scraping applications, especially when dealing with complex workflows or distributed systems. This section explores how message queues can enhance your web scraping architecture and improve efficiency.

1. What are Message Queues?

A message queue is a software component that allows different parts of an application (or different applications) to communicate asynchronously by sending and receiving messages. Messages are typically placed in a queue, where they are stored until a consumer retrieves and processes them.

Key Concepts:

- **Producer:** The component that sends messages to the queue.
- **Consumer:** The component that receives and processes messages from the queue.

- **Queue:** The buffer that stores messages until they are consumed.

2. Benefits for Web Scraping

- **Decoupling:** Message queues decouple different parts of your scraping pipeline, allowing them to operate independently and at different speeds.
- **Scalability:** Distribute scraping tasks across multiple consumers, improving scalability and fault tolerance.
- **Asynchronous Processing:** Enable asynchronous processing of tasks, such as data cleaning, transformation, or storage, without blocking the main scraping process.
- **Workflow Management:** Manage complex scraping workflows with multiple stages and dependencies.
- **Error Handling:** Handle errors gracefully by re-queueing failed tasks or routing them to specific error queues.

3. Popular Message Queues

- **RabbitMQ:** A robust and widely used open-source message broker that supports various messaging protocols.
- **Celery:** A distributed task queue that focuses on real-time operation and supports task scheduling.

- **Amazon SQS:** A fully managed message queuing service provided by AWS.
- **Google Cloud Pub/Sub:** A real-time messaging service offered by Google Cloud.

4. Integrating Message Queues with Web Scraping

- **Producer (Scraper):** The scraper acts as the producer, sending messages (e.g., URLs to scrape, scraped data) to the queue.
- **Consumers (Workers):** Separate worker processes or threads act as consumers, retrieving messages from the queue and performing tasks like data cleaning, processing, or storage.

5. Example: Using Celery for Asynchronous Data Processing

Python

```
# tasks.py (Celery tasks)

from celery import Celery


app = Celery('tasks', broker='pyamqp://guest@localhost//')  # Configure Celery
```

```python
@app.task

def process_data(data):

    # ... (code to process the data) ...


# scraper.py (main script)

from tasks import import process_data


# ... (scrape data) ...


# Send data to the queue for processing

process_data.delay(scraped_data)
```

In this example, Celery is used to define a task (process_data) that processes scraped data asynchronously. The scraper sends data to the queue using process_data.delay(), and Celery workers will retrieve and process the data in the background.

6. Choosing a Message Queue

Consider factors like:

- **Features:** Required messaging patterns, routing options, and supported protocols.
- **Scalability:** Ability to handle the volume of messages and desired throughput.
- **Reliability:** Durability of messages, fault tolerance, and message delivery guarantees.
- **Ease of Use:** Simplicity of setup, configuration, and integration with your existing infrastructure.

By incorporating message queues into your web scraping architecture, you can achieve greater scalability, decoupling, and asynchronous processing, leading to more efficient and robust scraping applications.

Cloud-Based Scraping with AWS Lambda or Google Cloud Functions

Cloud computing has revolutionized how we build and deploy applications, and web scraping is no exception. This section explores how to leverage cloud-based services like AWS Lambda or Google Cloud Functions to create scalable and cost-effective web scraping solutions.

1. Serverless Computing

AWS Lambda and Google Cloud Functions are examples of serverless computing platforms. They allow you to run code without provisioning or managing servers. You simply upload your code, and the platform takes care of executing it in response to events or triggers.

Key Benefits:

- **Scalability:** The platform automatically scales your code to handle varying workloads, ensuring high availability and performance.
- **Cost-Effectiveness:** You only pay for the compute time actually used, making it a cost-effective solution for intermittent or bursty workloads like web scraping.
- **Reduced Operational Overhead:** No need to manage servers, operating systems, or infrastructure.

2. AWS Lambda for Web Scraping

AWS Lambda allows you to run Python code in response to various events, including HTTP requests, scheduled events, or messages from other AWS services.

- **Steps:**
  - Create a Lambda function and upload your scraping code.
  - Package any necessary dependencies with your code.
  - Configure a trigger (e.g., an API Gateway endpoint, a scheduled event) to invoke your function.

- Lambda executes your code when triggered, fetching and processing data as needed.
- Store the scraped data in an AWS service like S3, DynamoDB, or RDS.

3. Google Cloud Functions for Web Scraping

Google Cloud Functions provide similar functionalities, allowing you to run Node.js, Python, Go, or Java code in a serverless environment.

- **Steps:**
  - Create a Cloud Function and deploy your scraping code.
  - Specify dependencies in your function's configuration.
  - Set up a trigger (e.g., an HTTP endpoint, a Cloud Storage event) to invoke the function.
  - Cloud Functions executes your code, scraping data and storing it in services like Cloud Storage, Cloud SQL, or Firestore.

4. Advantages of Cloud-Based Scraping

- **Scalability:** Handle large-scale scraping tasks with automatic scaling.

- **Cost-Efficiency:** Pay only for the compute time used.
- **Maintainability:** Simplified deployment and management of your scraping code.
- **Integration with Other Services:** Integrate with other cloud services for data storage, processing, and analysis.

5. Considerations

- **Execution Time Limits:** Serverless functions typically have execution time limits. For long-running scraping tasks, consider breaking them down into smaller functions or using alternative solutions.
- **Cold Starts:** The initial invocation of a serverless function might have a cold start latency. Optimize your code and minimize dependencies to reduce cold start times.
- **Vendor Lock-in:** Be aware of potential vendor lock-in when choosing a cloud provider.

6. Example: Scraping with AWS Lambda and API Gateway

- Create an AWS Lambda function with your scraping code.
- Configure an API Gateway endpoint to trigger the Lambda function.

- Send an HTTP request to the API Gateway endpoint.
- API Gateway invokes the Lambda function, which performs the scraping and returns the data.

By leveraging cloud-based serverless platforms like AWS Lambda or Google Cloud Functions, you can build scalable, cost-effective, and maintainable web scraping solutions that can handle demanding data extraction tasks.

Part V: Best Practices and Beyond

Chapter 13: Testing and Debugging

Writing Unit Tests for Your Scrapers

Testing is a critical practice in software development, and web scraping is no exception. Thorough testing ensures that your scraper works as expected, handles different scenarios correctly, and remains robust as websites evolve. This section focuses on writing unit tests for your scrapers, a fundamental technique for verifying the functionality of individual components.

Writing Unit Tests for Your Scrapers

Unit tests are automated tests that verify the behavior of small, isolated units of code, such as functions or methods. They help you catch errors early in the development process, improve code quality, and facilitate refactoring with confidence.

1. Benefits of Unit Testing

- **Early Error Detection:** Identify bugs and logic errors early in the development cycle, making them easier and cheaper to fix.
- **Improved Code Quality:** Encourage modular design, code clarity, and better separation of concerns.

- **Confidence in Refactoring:** Refactor your code with confidence, knowing that unit tests will catch any regressions or unintended changes in behavior.
- **Documentation:** Well-written unit tests serve as documentation, demonstrating how individual components are intended to work.
- **Regression Prevention:** Prevent regressions (reintroducing old bugs) when making changes or adding new features.

2. Unit Testing Frameworks

Python provides built-in frameworks for unit testing:

- unittest**:** A standard library module that provides a framework for organizing and running tests.
- pytest**:** A popular third-party library that offers a more concise and flexible approach to testing.

3. Writing Unit Tests with unittest

- **Create a Test Case:** Define a test class that inherits from unittest.TestCase.
- **Write Test Methods:** Write test methods that start with test_ and use assertion methods to verify expected outcomes.
- **Example:**

Python

```python
import unittest

from my_scraper import extract_product_data


class TestScraper(unittest.TestCase):

    def test_extract_product_data_valid_html(self):
        html = """
        <div class="product">
            <h2 class="title">Product Name</h2>
            <p class="price">$19.99</p>
        </div>
        """

        data = extract_product_data(html)
        self.assertEqual(data['title'], 'Product Name')
        self.assertEqual(data['price'], '$19.99')


    def test_extract_product_data_missing_price(self):
        html = """
```

```
<div class="product">

    <h2 class="title">Product Name</h2>

</div>
"""

    data = extract_product_data(html)

    self.assertIsNone(data['price'])  # Expecting price to
be None


if __name__ == '__main__':

    unittest.main()
```

4. Test-Driven Development (TDD)

TDD is a development approach where you write tests before writing the actual code. This helps you clarify requirements, design testable code, and ensure that your code meets the defined expectations.

5. Best Practices

- **Test Individual Units:** Focus on testing individual functions or methods in isolation.
- **Use Meaningful Test Names:** Use descriptive names that clearly indicate the purpose of the test.
- **Test Different Scenarios:** Test both positive and negative cases, including edge cases and potential errors.
- **Keep Tests Independent:** Tests should not depend on each other or on external factors.
- **Use Mocks or Fixtures:** Use mocks or fixtures to simulate external dependencies or data.

6. Continuous Integration

Integrate your unit tests into a continuous integration (CI) system to automatically run tests whenever you make changes to your code. This helps catch errors early and ensures that your scraper remains functional as you develop and maintain it.

By adopting unit testing practices and incorporating them into your web scraping workflow, you can significantly improve the quality, reliability, and maintainability of your scrapers.

Debugging Techniques for Common Scraping Issues

Web scraping can be prone to errors due to factors like website changes, network issues, or unexpected data formats. This section equips you with debugging techniques to identify and resolve common scraping issues effectively.

1. Common Scraping Issues

- **Incorrect Selectors:** CSS selectors or XPath expressions used to locate elements might be incorrect or outdated due to changes in the website's structure.
- **Network Errors:** Network connectivity problems, server errors, or timeouts can prevent your scraper from fetching web pages.
- **Data Extraction Errors:** The logic for extracting data from HTML or JSON might be flawed, leading to incorrect or missing values.
- **Anti-Scraping Measures:** Websites might employ anti-scraping techniques like rate limiting, IP blocking, or CAPTCHAs, hindering your scraping efforts.
- **Unexpected Data Formats:** The website might return data in an unexpected format or structure, causing parsing errors.

2. Debugging Techniques

- **Print Statements:** Insert print() statements to inspect variables, data structures, and the flow of your code.
- **Logging:** Use the logging module to record events, errors, and warnings, providing a detailed trace of your scraper's execution.
- **Interactive Debuggers:** Utilize Python's built-in debugger (pdb) or IDE debugging tools to step through your code, set breakpoints, and examine variables.
- **Browser Developer Tools:** Inspect the website's HTML structure, network requests, and JavaScript console using your browser's developer tools to understand how the website is loading and rendering content.
- **Error Handling:** Implement try-except blocks to catch exceptions and handle them gracefully, providing informative error messages.
- **Testing:** Write unit tests to verify the behavior of individual components and identify potential errors early in the development process.
- **Online Tools:** Use online tools like the W3C Markup Validation Service to check for errors in HTML or CSS that might affect scraping.

3. Example: Debugging with Print Statements

```python
Python
import requests
from bs4 import BeautifulSoup

def scrape_product(url):
    response = requests.get(url)
    print(f"Status Code: {response.status_code}")  # Check the status code

    soup = BeautifulSoup(response.content, 'html.parser')
    title = soup.find('h1', class_='product-title')
    print(f"Title Element: {title}")  # Inspect the title element

    if title:
        return title.text
    else:
        return None
```

In this example, print() statements are used to check the response status code and inspect the title element, helping you identify potential issues with fetching the page or locating the desired data.

4. Debugging Tips

- **Isolate the Issue:** Try to isolate the specific part of your code that is causing the error.
- **Simplify the Problem:** Create a minimal reproducible example that demonstrates the issue.
- **Check for Website Changes:** Websites frequently update their structure, which can break your scraper. Use browser developer tools to inspect the updated HTML.
- **Read Error Messages Carefully:** Pay close attention to error messages, as they often provide valuable clues about the source of the problem.
- **Consult Documentation:** Refer to the documentation of the libraries and tools you are using to understand their behavior and troubleshoot issues.

By applying these debugging techniques and following best practices, you can effectively identify and resolve common scraping issues, ensuring that your scrapers remain robust and reliable.

Logging and Monitoring Your Scrapers

Logging and monitoring are essential practices for maintaining the health and performance of your web scrapers. Logging provides a record of events, errors, and other relevant information during your scraper's execution. Monitoring allows you to track key metrics and identify potential issues or bottlenecks.

1. Benefits of Logging

- **Error Tracking:** Log errors and exceptions to identify the cause of problems and facilitate debugging.
- **Progress Monitoring:** Track the progress of your scraper, including the number of pages scraped, items processed, and data extracted.
- **Debugging:** Use log messages to inspect variables, data structures, and the flow of your code, aiding in debugging.
- **Auditing:** Maintain an audit trail of your scraper's activities, including when it ran, what data it accessed, and any actions it performed.
- **Performance Analysis:** Log timing information to identify performance bottlenecks or areas for optimization.

2. Python's logging Module

Python's built-in logging module provides a flexible framework for logging messages from your applications.

- **Log Levels:** Use different log levels (DEBUG, INFO, WARNING, ERROR, CRITICAL) to categorize messages based on their severity.
- **Log Handlers:** Configure handlers to direct log messages to various destinations, such as the console, files, or external logging services.
- **Log Formatting:** Customize the format of log messages to include relevant information like timestamps, log levels, and source file names.

3. Example: Logging with logging

Python

```python
import logging


# Configure logging

logging.basicConfig(filename='scraper.log',
level=logging.INFO,

                    format='%(asctime)s - %(levelname)s -
%(message)s')


def scrape_page(url):
```

```
try:

    # ... (scrape data) ...

    logging.info(f"Successfully scraped {url}")

except Exception as e:

    logging.error(f"Error scraping {url}: {e}")
```

This example configures logging to write messages to a file named scraper.log. It logs informational messages about successful scraping and error messages for any exceptions encountered.

4. Monitoring

Monitoring involves tracking key metrics and performance indicators to gain insights into your scraper's health and identify potential issues.

- **Metrics to Monitor:**
  - **Scraping Speed:** Track the number of pages scraped per minute or hour.
  - **Success Rate:** Monitor the percentage of successful scraping attempts.
  - **Error Rate:** Track the number and types of errors encountered.

- Data Volume: Monitor the amount of data extracted and stored.
- Resource Usage: Track CPU usage, memory consumption, and network bandwidth.
- **Monitoring Tools:**
  - CloudWatch (AWS): Monitor logs and metrics for AWS Lambda functions.
  - Cloud Logging (Google Cloud): Monitor logs and metrics for Google Cloud Functions.
  - Prometheus: An open-source monitoring system with a flexible query language.
  - Grafana: A data visualization and monitoring tool that can be used with Prometheus or other data sources.

5. Alerting

Set up alerts to notify you when specific events occur or metrics exceed predefined thresholds. This allows you to proactively address issues and prevent potential disruptions.

6. Best Practices

- **Log Relevant Information:** Include relevant context in your log messages, such as URLs, timestamps, and data samples.

- **Use Appropriate Log Levels:** Categorize messages using appropriate log levels to filter and prioritize information.
- **Monitor Key Metrics:** Identify and track the most important metrics for your scraper's performance and health.
- **Set Up Alerts:** Configure alerts to notify you of critical events or performance issues.

By effectively utilizing logging and monitoring, you can gain valuable insights into your scraper's operation, identify potential problems, and ensure its long-term stability and performance.

Chapter 14: Web Scraping Best Practices

Code Style and Organization

As you gain experience with web scraping, adopting best practices becomes crucial for writing clean, maintainable, and efficient code. This section focuses on code style and organization, essential elements for creating professional-grade web scraping projects.

Code Style and Organization

Consistent code style and well-organized code are vital for readability, collaboration, and long-term maintainability. They make your code easier to understand, debug, and update, whether you're working solo or as part of a team.

1. Why Code Style Matters

- **Readability:** Consistent indentation, spacing, and naming conventions make your code easier to read and comprehend.
- **Maintainability:** Well-structured code with clear organization is easier to modify, debug, and extend over time.
- **Collaboration:** A consistent style facilitates collaboration, allowing multiple developers to work on the same project seamlessly.

- **Professionalism:** Adhering to code style guidelines demonstrates professionalism and attention to detail.

2. Python Style Guide (PEP 8)

PEP 8 (Python Enhancement Proposal 8) is the official style guide for Python code. It provides recommendations on various aspects of code style, including:

- **Indentation:** Use 4 spaces per indentation level.
- **Naming Conventions:**
    - Variables and functions: lower_case_with_underscores
    - Classes: CamelCase
    - Constants: UPPER_CASE_WITH_UNDERSCORES
- **Line Length:** Limit lines to a maximum of 79 characters.
- **Whitespace:** Use whitespace effectively to improve readability (e.g., around operators, after commas).
- **Comments:** Write clear and concise comments to explain your code.

3. Code Organization

- **Modular Design:** Break down your scraper into smaller, reusable modules or functions with clear responsibilities.
- **Separation of Concerns:** Separate different functionalities, such as data extraction, cleaning, processing, and storage, into distinct modules or classes.
- **File Structure:** Organize your project with a clear file structure, grouping related modules or using a hierarchical structure.
- **Project Layout:** Consider using a common project layout, such as:

my_scraper/

   scraper.py # Main script

   modules/

      data_extraction.py

      data_cleaning.py

      data_storage.py

   config.py # Configuration settings

   requirements.txt # Project dependencies

4. Tools for Code Style and Organization

- **Linters:** Tools like pylint or flake8 analyze your code for style violations and potential errors.
- **Code Formatters:** Tools like black or autopep8 automatically format your code to conform to PEP 8 guidelines.
- **IDE Support:** Most IDEs provide built-in support for code style checking and formatting.

5. Example: Well-Organized Scraper

Python

```python
# scraper.py

from modules import data_extraction, data_cleaning,
data_storage


def main():
    # ... (load configuration) ...
    for url in urls:
        raw_data = data_extraction.scrape_page(url)
        cleaned_data = data_cleaning.clean_data(raw_data)
```

```python
    data_storage.store_data(cleaned_data)


if __name__ == "__main__":

    main()
```

This example demonstrates a well-organized scraper with modular design and separation of concerns.

6. Continuous Improvement

- **Code Reviews:** Conduct code reviews with peers to identify potential style issues or areas for improvement.
- **Refactoring:** Regularly refactor your code to improve its structure, readability, and maintainability.
- **Stay Updated:** Keep up-to-date with the latest PEP 8 recommendations and best practices for code style and organization.

By consistently applying code style guidelines and maintaining a well-organized codebase, you can create professional-grade web scraping projects that are easier to read, maintain, and collaborate on.

Performance Optimization Tips

Efficient web scraping involves optimizing your code to minimize resource usage and maximize data extraction speed. This section provides practical tips for improving the performance of your web scrapers.

1. Efficient Libraries and Tools

- **Choose fast libraries:**
  - **Requests:** While versatile, consider alternatives like aiohttp for asynchronous requests, which can significantly improve performance for I/O-bound tasks.
  - **Parsing:** Use efficient HTML/XML parsing libraries like lxml for faster processing.
- **Browser Automation:** If using browser automation, optimize browser settings and consider headless mode for faster execution.

2. Reduce Network Overhead

- **Minimize Requests:** Only request the essential pages and data. Avoid unnecessary requests or fetching redundant information.
- **Caching:** Implement caching mechanisms to store previously fetched data, avoiding redundant requests to the same URLs.

- **Compression:** Request compressed responses (e.g., gzip) to reduce data transfer size.

3. Optimize Data Extraction

- **Targeted Scraping:** Use precise CSS selectors or XPath expressions to extract only the necessary data, avoiding unnecessary DOM traversal.
- **Avoid Regular Expressions (When Possible):** While powerful, regular expressions can be computationally expensive. Use them judiciously and consider alternatives like string methods when appropriate.
- **Efficient Data Structures:** Use appropriate data structures (e.g., dictionaries, sets) for efficient data storage and retrieval.

4. Concurrency and Parallelism

- **Threading/Multiprocessing:** For CPU-bound tasks, use multiprocessing to utilize multiple CPU cores. For I/O-bound tasks, threading can improve concurrency.
- **Asynchronous Programming:** Leverage asynchronous programming (asyncio) to efficiently handle I/O-bound operations and maximize concurrency.

5. Code Optimization

- **Profiling:** Use profiling tools to identify performance bottlenecks in your code and focus optimization efforts on the most critical areas.
- **Avoid Unnecessary Computations:** Minimize redundant calculations or loops. Store intermediate results if they are reused multiple times.
- **Optimize Loops:** Use vectorized operations (e.g., with NumPy) or list comprehensions for faster loop execution.

6. Data Storage and Management

- **Efficient Databases:** Choose a database (SQL or NoSQL) that is optimized for your data structure, query patterns, and scalability needs.
- **Indexing:** Use appropriate indexing in your database to speed up data retrieval.
- **Data Compression:** Consider compressing data before storing it to reduce storage space and improve transfer speeds.

7. Monitoring and Optimization

- **Monitoring:** Monitor your scraper's performance (e.g., scraping speed, error rate) to identify areas for improvement.
- **Logging:** Use logging to track events, errors, and timing information, aiding in performance analysis.

- **Continuous Optimization:** Regularly review and optimize your code based on performance data and evolving requirements.

By applying these performance optimization techniques, you can create web scrapers that run faster, consume fewer resources, and handle larger datasets efficiently.

Ethical Considerations and Responsible Scraping

Web scraping, while a powerful tool for data extraction, raises ethical considerations that need careful attention. Responsible scraping involves respecting website owners, users, and the broader internet ecosystem. This section outlines key ethical principles and best practices for conducting web scraping in a responsible and sustainable manner.

1. Respect Website Terms of Service

- **Review Terms:** Carefully review the website's terms of service or acceptable use policy. Look for clauses related to data scraping, automated access, and usage restrictions.
- **Explicit Prohibitions:** Some websites explicitly prohibit scraping or automated data collection. Respect these restrictions to avoid legal issues or access revocation.

- **Rate Limits:** Adhere to any specified rate limits to avoid overloading the server or being perceived as a malicious actor.

2. Adhere to robots.txt

- **Check robots.txt:** Before scraping, check the website's robots.txt file, which provides instructions to web robots (including scrapers) about which parts of the site should not be accessed.
- **Respect Directives:** Follow the directives in robots.txt, such as Disallow and Crawl-delay, to avoid accessing restricted content or overloading the server.

3. Minimize Impact on Website Performance

- **Rate Limiting:** Implement delays between requests to avoid overwhelming the server with traffic.
- **Off-Peak Scraping:** Consider scheduling your scraping activities during off-peak hours to minimize impact on website performance.
- **Targeted Scraping:** Only scrape the data you need and avoid unnecessary requests.

4. Protect User Privacy

- **Personal Data:** Avoid scraping sensitive personal data (e.g., names, addresses, emails) unless explicitly permitted or necessary for a legitimate purpose with user consent.

- **Data Security:** Implement appropriate security measures to protect the data you collect, especially if it includes personal information.
- **Compliance:** Be aware of and comply with relevant data privacy regulations like GDPR and CCPA.

5. Transparency and Identification

- **Identify Yourself:** Use a descriptive User-Agent header that identifies your scraper and provides contact information.
- **Transparency:** Be transparent about your scraping activities if contacting the website owner or requesting access to data.

6. Avoid Copyright Infringement

- **Copyright Laws:** Respect copyright laws and avoid scraping copyrighted content (e.g., articles, images) without permission.
- **Fair Use:** Understand the principles of fair use, but be cautious when scraping copyrighted material, as fair use is a complex legal area.

7. Community and Ecosystem

- **Open Source:** Consider contributing to open-source scraping tools or libraries.

- **Responsible Disclosure:** If you discover vulnerabilities or security issues on a website while scraping, responsibly disclose them to the website owner.
- **Avoid Harm:** Do not use web scraping for malicious activities or to spread misinformation.

8. Continuous Evaluation

- **Reassess Practices:** Regularly review your scraping practices and adapt them as needed to ensure ethical and responsible behavior.
- **Stay Informed:** Stay informed about evolving best practices, legal developments, and ethical considerations in the web scraping field.

By adhering to these ethical principles and best practices, you can contribute to a sustainable web scraping ecosystem that respects website owners, protects user privacy, and promotes responsible data extraction.

Chapter 15: Future Trends in Web Scraping

The Rise of Serverless Computing

The field of web scraping is constantly evolving, driven by advancements in technology and the ever-changing landscape of the web.[1] This chapter explores future trends in web scraping, starting with the rise of serverless computing and its impact on how we build and deploy scraping solutions.

The Rise of Serverless Computing

Serverless computing is a cloud computing model where you can run code without provisioning or managing servers.[2] Providers like AWS Lambda and Google Cloud Functions allow you to execute code in response to events or triggers, abstracting away the underlying infrastructure.[3] This paradigm shift is transforming web scraping in several ways.[4]

1. Scalability and Elasticity

Serverless platforms automatically scale your code to handle fluctuating workloads.[5] This is particularly beneficial for web scraping, where demands can vary significantly depending on the number of pages to scrape, the frequency of updates, and the complexity of data extraction.

- **Automatic Scaling:** No need to manually provision or configure servers.[6] The platform dynamically allocates resources as needed.[7]
- **Cost-Efficiency:** Pay only for the compute time actually used, making it cost-effective for intermittent or bursty workloads like web scraping.[8]

2. Simplified Deployment and Management

Serverless computing simplifies the deployment and management of web scraping applications.[9]

- **Focus on Code:** You can focus on writing your scraping logic without worrying about server management, operating systems, or infrastructure.[10]
- **Automated Deployment:** Deploy your code with ease, often using simple command-line tools or web interfaces.
- **Reduced Operational Overhead:** No need to handle server maintenance, security updates, or scaling infrastructure.[11]

3. Integration with Other Cloud Services

Serverless functions seamlessly integrate with other cloud services, creating a powerful ecosystem for web scraping.[12]

- **Data Storage:** Store scraped data in cloud storage services like AWS S3, Google Cloud Storage, or databases like DynamoDB and Cloud SQL.[13]
- **API Gateways:** Trigger serverless functions through API Gateways, allowing you to create web scraping APIs.
- **Message Queues:** Use message queues like SQS or Pub/Sub to decouple scraping tasks and improve scalability.
- **Data Processing and Analysis:** Integrate with data processing services like AWS Glue or Google Cloud Dataflow for further analysis and transformation of scraped data.[14]

4. Use Cases for Serverless Scraping

- **Scheduled Scraping:** Run serverless functions on a schedule (e.g., daily, hourly) to scrape data periodically.[15]
- **Event-Driven Scraping:** Trigger scraping functions in response to events like new product listings, price changes, or social media updates.[16]
- **Real-time Scraping:** Handle real-time data streams or updates using serverless functions that process data as it becomes available.

- **Microservices Architecture:** Decompose complex scraping tasks into smaller, independent serverless functions that interact with each other.

5. Challenges and Considerations

- **Execution Time Limits:** Serverless functions typically have execution time limits.[17] For long-running scraping tasks, consider breaking them down or using alternative solutions.
- **Cold Starts:** The initial invocation of a serverless function might have a cold start latency.[18] Optimize your code and dependencies to minimize this.
- **Vendor Lock-in:** Be aware of potential vendor lock-in when choosing a serverless platform.

6. Future Outlook

Serverless computing is expected to play an increasingly important role in web scraping, enabling more scalable, cost-effective, and maintainable solutions. The integration with other cloud services and the growing ecosystem of tools and frameworks will further enhance the capabilities of serverless scraping.

By embracing serverless computing, web scraping developers can focus on their core scraping logic, leverage the scalability and cost-efficiency of the cloud, and build robust solutions that adapt to the evolving demands of data extraction.

AI and Machine Learning in Web Scraping

Artificial intelligence (AI) and machine learning (ML) are rapidly transforming the field of web scraping, enabling more intelligent, adaptable, and efficient data extraction. This section explores how AI and ML are being applied to overcome challenges and enhance various aspects of web scraping.

1. Intelligent Data Extraction

- **Natural Language Processing (NLP):** NLP techniques can be used to analyze text content on web pages, identify relevant information, and extract data with greater accuracy.
    - **Named Entity Recognition (NER):** Extract named entities like people, organizations, locations, and products from web pages.
    - **Sentiment Analysis:** Analyze the sentiment expressed in text content, such as product reviews or social media comments.
    - **Topic Modeling:** Identify the main topics or themes discussed on a web page or across a collection of pages.

- **Computer Vision:** Computer vision techniques can be used to analyze images and videos on web pages, extract information from visual elements, and solve image-based CAPTCHAs.
  - **Image Classification:** Categorize images based on their content (e.g., product images, logos).
  - **Object Detection:** Identify and locate specific objects within images (e.g., faces, products).
  - **Optical Character Recognition (OCR):** Extract text from images, including distorted text in CAPTCHAs.

2. Automated Pattern Recognition

Machine learning can be used to automatically identify patterns and structures in web pages, enabling more robust and adaptable scraping.

- **Website Structure Learning:** Train ML models to learn the structure of websites and identify relevant data elements, even if the structure changes over time.
- **Data Format Recognition:** Automatically recognize different data formats (e.g., tables, lists, key-value pairs) and adapt the scraping logic accordingly.

- **Dynamic Content Handling:** Predict and handle dynamic content changes using ML models that learn how websites update information.

3. Anti-Scraping Circumvention

AI and ML can help overcome anti-scraping measures employed by websites.

- **CAPTCHA Solving:** Train ML models to solve CAPTCHAs with high accuracy, using techniques like image recognition and deep learning.
- **Bot Detection Evasion:** Develop strategies to evade bot detection mechanisms by mimicking human-like behavior or generating realistic user interactions.

4. Scraping Efficiency and Optimization

- **Resource Allocation:** Use ML to optimize resource allocation for scraping, prioritizing high-value targets and adapting scraping frequency based on website updates.
- **Performance Prediction:** Predict scraping performance and identify potential bottlenecks using ML models that analyze historical data.

5. Ethical Considerations

- **Bias and Fairness:** Be aware of potential biases in training data and ensure that AI-powered scraping systems do not perpetuate or amplify discriminatory practices.
- **Transparency and Explainability:** Strive for transparency in how AI is used in scraping and ensure that decisions made by AI systems are explainable.
- **Data Privacy:** Use AI responsibly to protect user privacy and avoid collecting or processing sensitive data without consent.

6. Future Outlook

AI and ML will continue to play an increasingly important role in web scraping, enabling more intelligent, adaptable, and efficient data extraction. As these technologies advance, we can expect even more sophisticated solutions for overcoming scraping challenges and extracting valuable insights from the web.

By embracing AI and ML, web scraping developers can create more robust, adaptable, and intelligent scrapers that can handle the complexities of the modern web and extract valuable data with greater accuracy and efficiency.

The Evolving Landscape of Web Technologies

Web technologies are in a constant state of flux, driven by innovation, user expectations, and the demand for richer online experiences. This continuous evolution presents both challenges and opportunities for web scraping. This section examines how the changing landscape of web technologies is impacting the field of web scraping.

1. The Rise of JavaScript Frameworks

Modern web development heavily relies on JavaScript frameworks and libraries like React, Angular, and Vue.js. These frameworks enable the creation of dynamic, interactive single-page applications (SPAs) where content is rendered on the client-side.

- **Challenges for Scraping:** Traditional scraping techniques that focus on static HTML struggle to extract data from SPAs where content is generated by JavaScript.
- **Solutions:** Browser automation tools like Selenium and Playwright become essential for scraping SPAs, allowing you to execute JavaScript and render dynamic content.

2. Increased Use of APIs

Websites are increasingly offering APIs (Application Programming Interfaces) as a structured way to access their data. APIs provide a programmatic interface for interacting with web services, enabling efficient and standardized data retrieval.

- **Opportunities for Scraping:** APIs often provide a more efficient and reliable way to access data compared to web scraping, as they return data in structured formats like JSON or XML.
- **Shift Towards API Integration:** Web scraping might involve integrating with APIs alongside traditional scraping techniques to access a wider range of data.

3. Progressive Web Apps (PWAs)

PWAs combine the best of web and mobile app experiences, offering features like offline access, push notifications, and native-like performance.

- **Scraping Considerations:** PWAs might employ service workers and caching mechanisms that can affect how data is fetched and rendered.
- **Adaptation of Techniques:** Scraping PWAs might require adapting existing techniques or using tools that can handle the unique characteristics of PWAs.

4. WebAssembly (Wasm)

WebAssembly is a binary instruction format that allows code written in languages like C, C++, and Rust to run in web browsers.

- **Performance Improvements:** Wasm can significantly improve the performance of web applications, potentially making scraping more challenging if complex logic is executed client-side.
- **New Tools and Techniques:** Scraping Wasm-based applications might require new tools or techniques to understand and interact with the compiled code.

5. Serverless Computing

Serverless computing platforms like AWS Lambda and Google Cloud Functions are gaining popularity for web scraping.

- **Scalability and Cost-Efficiency:** Serverless functions allow you to run scraping code without managing servers, providing scalability and cost-efficiency.
- **Integration with Cloud Services:** Integrate serverless functions with other cloud services for data storage, processing, and analysis.

6. AI and Machine Learning

AI and ML are being increasingly applied to enhance web scraping capabilities.

- **Intelligent Data Extraction:** Use NLP and computer vision to extract data with greater accuracy and handle unstructured content.
- **Automated Pattern Recognition:** Train ML models to learn website structures and adapt to changes dynamically.

7. Ethical and Legal Considerations

The evolving web landscape also brings new ethical and legal considerations for web scraping.

- **Data Privacy:** Respect user privacy and comply with data protection regulations like GDPR and CCPA.
- **Website Terms:** Adhere to website terms of service and robots.txt rules.
- **Responsible Scraping:** Minimize impact on website performance and avoid malicious activities.

By staying informed about these evolving web technologies and adapting their scraping techniques accordingly, developers can continue to extract valuable data from the web and build robust solutions that meet the challenges of the ever-changing online world.